SPANISH ACADEMY SOCCER COACHING

120 Practices from the Coaches of Real Madrid, Atlético Madrid and Athletic Bilbao

Written by

Jon Moreno   Santiago Esposito   Jose F. Lopez   Iván M. Campos

Published by

Spanish Academy Soccer Coaching
120 Practices from the Coaches of Real Madrid, Atlético Madrid and Athletic Bilbao

First Published August 2012 by SoccerTutor.com

Info@soccertutor.com | www.SoccerTutor.com
UK: 0208 1234 007 | **US:** (305) 767 4443 | **ROTW:** +44 208 1234 007

ISBN 978-0-9566752-6-2

Original Spanish Publishers
Abfutbol ©, All Rights Reserved.

Spanish to English Translation
Abby Parkhouse - abbyparkhouse@yahoo.co.uk

Edited by
Alex Fitzgerald - SoccerTutor.com

Cover Design by
Alex Macrides, Think Out Of The Box Ltd.
Email: design@thinkootb.com Tel: +44 (0) 208 144 3550

Diagrams
Diagram designs by SoccerTutor.com. All the diagrams in this book have been created using SoccerTutor.com Tactics Manager Software available from
www.SoccerTutor.com

Note: While every effort has been made to ensure the technical accuracy of the content of this book, neither the author nor publishers can accept any responsibility for any injury or loss sustained as a result of the use of this material.

CONTENTS

THE SPANISH COACHING PHILOSOPHY

Technical training is the foundation of a footballer's development. Young players must learn these techniques in the early stages of their footballing life.

This technical base that is formed enables players to participate properly in the game, combining with their teammates. Passing, receiving and dribbling are fundamental skills that any young player should possess in order to progress.

Technique is obviously the most important aspect but without tactics is no use to anybody. There is a big difference between a highly skilled individual and a complete football player.

If a player does not make his skills available to the group and his decisions are outside the context of the game he is unable to play successfully in this sport.

A player's technical capacity allows them to "execute" the necessary changes to "resolve" a situation within a game and this is the objective of combining technical and tactical training.

With the disappearance of street football, schools play a key role in technical training. With less practice hours available now there is a need to increase the quality of teaching to gain a better understanding in less time.

This book should serve as a reference to aid you in designing training drills which help improve players technically.

We hope that it helps!

PRACTICE FORMAT

There are 4 different Spanish academy coaches each with a range of practices.

Each practice includes clear diagrams with supporting training notes such as:

- Name of Practice
- Objective of Practice
- Coaching Points of Practice
- Variations or Progression of Practice (if applicable)

KEY

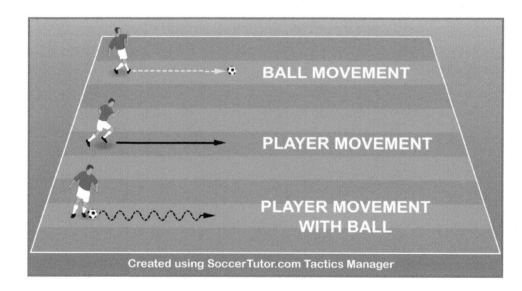

BALL MOVEMENT

PLAYER MOVEMENT

PLAYER MOVEMENT WITH BALL

Created using SoccerTutor.com Tactics Manager

CHAPTER 1

JON MORENO MARTÍNEZ

Athletic Bilbao
Academy Coach

ATHLETIC BILBAO ACADEMY COACH PROFILE

Jon MORENO MARTÍNEZ
Athletic Bilbao Academy Coach

- National football coach (level III)
- Bachelors Degree in Physical and Sport Education
- Master of physical training in football. (APF-RFEF)
- Master in High Performance Sports (COE)

Jon Moreno focuses on technical work and employs tactics into the different stages of training.

INTRODUCTION

"Grassroots football is not competitive football but football training"

This fundamental premise should be taken into account for the technical and tactical work during the different stages of training. The results and ratings are consequences of the work carried out and we must instil this into our youngsters in grassroots football. We must not forget the principal training objectives to train people to play football at any level, respect the values of the sport, the game and the opposition and above all enjoy the practice more than the result.

Formative football always triggers debates. Youth teams are criticised because they do not all become first team players. One of the problems could be the lack of continuity and progression in the groundwork and the lack of adaptation of football development to the ability of the child.

"Slow and steady wins the race. There is no need to rush the training"

Footballers are born, but have to work extremely hard to reach the highest level. We must not rush the formative stages to reach an imaginary destination. Competitive excellence comes when you reach the "senior" stage, and although there, you still need to carry on training as you can never stop learning, progressing and improving. Continuity is the cornerstone of grassroots football.

"The secret to success in football is in the training"

Phrases such as, *"the more I train, the more luck I have"* (Luis Aragonés), serve as a guide to the way forward. You must train often and well in order to progress. This training should address the essentials of the game which is to adapt effectively and act at the opportune moment. As such, training should be based on both technical and tactical work without the need for separation as technique and tactics never manifest themselves separately during a game.

"Training should always have competitive characteristics"

Excessive competitiveness stalls progression in grassroots football. We should not forget that the young player is not a footballer but a youngster who plays football. Many coaches/teachers forget this, and try to transfer senior training drills onto their pupils, don't - they are the age they are, are in the condition they are in and have the ability that they have.

The football, the training and the drills must be adapted to the young player, and not the other way around. It is imperative that you plan, structure and organize the content of the training for the specific stages of football development. The objective is to develop their abilities progressively and ensure that the training ground is a place of learning, fun (without forgetting the competition) and education (in sport as well as personal). We first need to train them as people before we train them as footballers. What we should never create are obligations and frustrations that will discourage the child. All of this should not separate us from the ultimate aim- training to compete. The training should be competitive, starting with the basics of the game. The nature of the competition should not be to win in training or in competitive matches, but to learn to participate constructively, to work, learn the rules of the game, handle situations, learn movement and game situations.

Should football be taught the same to all categories of players?

The answer is simple but complicated to apply. There are various views on what should be taught in training. Football as a game is the same in all categories, what is not the same is the abilities of the youngsters in their different stages of development. There is content that we should work on in each stage but which should always be tailored to the individual and collective skills of the team. A generalised and simple proposal for a phased development could be the following:

	Ages 8-9	Ages 10-11	Ages 12-13	Ages 14-15	Youth
Technique	Individual technique Ball control	Individual technique Team technique Ball drills	Individual technique Team technique Individual/team drills	Team technique Systems drills	Individual technique Positioning drills
Tactics	Specific situations 1v0, 1v1, 2v2 Practice matches in smaller numbers	Principals of attacking and defending Specific situations 2-3v1, 4v2	Principals of attacking and defending Specific situations 5v3, 6v4	Principals of attacking and defending Specific situations 7v5, 8v6	Game plans and style Specific situations 8v8, 10v10
Competitive	Football games	Attack and defensive situations Beginners set pieces	Lines Improve set pieces	Systems Set pieces	Marking Systems Set pieces
Opposition	Without opposition	Passive opposition	No support	Superior	Equal
Objectives	Learning Provide technical resources	Assimilation and adaptation. Enrich technical-tactical drills	Improve technical-tactical drills	Develop the technical-tactical drills. Mechanization and effectiveness in games.	Advanced technical-tactical drills. Efficiency in competition.
Phases	Learning the movements	Learning movement and game situations	Adapting movement to different game situations	Mastering the movement and adapting to competitive situations	Integrating the movements into competitive situations.

Contemporary football is in a continuous state of evolution. This means that training models continually need to adapt to competitive requirements although the principals of the game remain the same.

How to train may change but what to achieve in training should not vary. All of the factors in football ensure that the training of the elite in football in continuously progressing and adapting, but at grassroots level it should not.

The training models, therefore, have to change depending on the coaches/trainers and categories and, above all, the ability of the players.

"I never teach my pupils, I only attempt to provide the conditions in which they can learn". (Albert Einstein)

How to train, the so called "method", is particular to each club, to each team and to each coach/trainer, but we cannot ignore that it is the child that has to learn how, when and where to perform. We need to provide them with good conditions so that they can provide solutions to the different situations that may arise during a game and guide them.

"Learning is not becoming able to repeat the same gesture, but to give the situation an appropriate response through different means". (Merleu-Ponty, 1942)

Analytical technical executions without a specific tactical situation provide a lack of meaning in the early stages of development. In the early stages of grassroots football, we should present specific technical situations aimed at specific tactical situations: Ball control during play, dribbling to push forward etc.

The objective is to create intelligent, autonomous, creative and thoughtful players (not robots who will do exactly what the coach dictates).

In short, training the young player is the protagonist and the objective. The coach and the whole environment should be completely at their service, impressing upon them the ability to learn and adapt, develop their personality and giving them every chance to train and compete with all of the necessary factors in place to help them perform.

The objective of the coach is to stimulate and motivate the young player to help them improve.

Results will be seen in the mid to long term, and the work should be progressive and adapted as much to an individual's characteristics as to those of the team as a whole.

Therefore, **PATIENCE** is the key.

FROM TECHNIQUE TO TACTICS, FROM TACTICS TO TECHNIQUE

"The technique supports the tactics, from the decision to the execution".

This phrase can guide us on the indivisibility of the two most crucial factors in football. All game action (execution) is preceded by a tactical decision in respect to each momentary game situation. Therefore, this idea should prevail in training when designing drills. We think and we execute so we can go back and rethink.

Technique is the means of executing all tactical and strategic processes. Tactics and technique relate to the effective use of the appropriate technical move at the right time to achieve a specific objective. Technique is the execution of the decision making process. Therefore, technique (execution) is supported by the tactics (decision making).

"Football starts in the head, passes through the body and down to the feet, never the other way around".

Starting from here, we can design exercises and drills that can guide football training on the importance of thinking before acting. In football they must learn decision making skills to act at the opportune moment, so we must mould thoughtful players, not obedient players.

"Playing with the ball is not the same as knowing what to do with it".

To play football, it is indispensable to have the ability to make decisions and the ability to carry them out, to address and respond to situations during a game. You continually make decisions whilst playing using a motor response: without the ability to execute these decisions, you will not be able to find a solution and use the tactical thinking in a game situation. Technical implementation by the players is governed and defined by the games regulations which covers and is responsible for all technical actions within the game.

"The better the technical ability, the better the footballer's resources to find solutions to tactical situations within the game".

Both are essential for football performance. The decision making should have an effective motor response and the motor execution must be well timed in order to be effective. It all unites in a collective sense. This is why tactics and technique are so united and should be trained together.

Therefore, we should not separate the technical and tactical training.

"Football is surprising, you need to be able to adapt to uncertainty and respond quickly and effectively to the situations that arise".

One of the most important aspects in the technical/tactical development of a young player is the encouragement of creativity and autonomy, promoting improvisation, the ability to break through, magic and natural talent - that they can also train, improve and hone their abilities with good planning starting at the grassroots level.

"Talent without effort is good for nothing". (Javier Imbroda)

The beauty in football is linked to the concept of the perfect execution, quality, talent and efficient service. Talent resides in creativity. Talent is an innate quality, but creativity has to be nurtured. Talent is the ability to foresee and anticipate future action (tactics), and have the ball in the optimal position to be played by either yourself or one of your teammates. To fake, dummy and control the ball or play one touch football are key to attacking situations. In defence, intensity, positioning and acting at the right moment are key skills.

Deciding when and how is the key part of the decision making process. The dummy, dribbling and deception are all indispensable ways of wrong footing your opponent.

TECHNIQUE

Technique is much about the execution of the perfect body shape. It is the tools and the support of both the tactics and the game. There are 3 factors that condition technique: skill, experience and talent (ability, the ability to learn and natural ability).

Training should stimulate the desire of children to learn and improve, awaking their talent through autonomy and creativity.

Why should you enhance the technical work?

Because technique is the means of executing any individual or team skill during a game and individual technique benefits the team as a whole.

How?

1. By knowing the capabilities and limitations of the group that we are training.
2. Distinguishing between offensive and defensive techniques, with and without the ball, individually and as a team (without forgetting the goalkeeper).
3. The exercises should allow everyone to participate, be comprehensive and specific, always ensuring quality in their execution.

When?

ALWAYS. Technique is present at every moment during a game and we should take this into account.

Exercises aimed at improving a specific or general skill must be present even during the warm up, throughout the drills and during the cooling down period.

TACTICS

The key is decision making; the ability to make a decision as quickly as possible and have the appropriate motor response to stimulate it during a game. Effective tactics are based on making the best decision at the appropriate time and place. In football you are continually making decisions.

Tactics and technique relate to the effective execution of the relevant action at the opportune moment. Technique supports the tactics and this is why they should be trained simultaneously. Tactics are about anticipating what is going to happen and being prepared to resolve the situation.

We should nurture the decision making capacity in all areas of training supplying problems that need to be solved (not solve the problems).

Tactical work should also stimulate creativity, autonomy and mental speed. The tactical progression should be adapted to the number of players and the amount of space. You must train the realities of the game, ensuring the essence of the game is there and all work should be geared towards this aim. All of the tasks should be played against opposition (progressing from passive to real) to create decision making situations.

Another elemental factor in improving decision making is peripheral vision, defined as the ability to foresee, see, look, analyse and solve the time-space relationships of teammates and opponents in respect of the ball and give an effective motor response based on prior experience (Moreno, J.). This ability should be trained to enhance decision making resources.

In summary, technique and tactics are linked and the training format should recognize this. All technical analytical tasks should be approached from a decision making view point.

FACTORS THAT INFLUENCE THE PERFORMANCE OF THE YOUNG FOOTBALLER

Performance in football is influenced by a number of factors that are all intertwined yet independent of each other. They all depend on each other and altering one can also modify another. Consequently, formative training should include all of the factors both in conjunction with each other and independently, and should also be integrated into each task.

The factors that affect performance in football are the following:

1. **Physical condition:** fitness and the capacity for physical work.

2. **Physical abilities** (basic and specific), **and physiology** (each individual players potential).

3. **Technical capacity:** execution of actions and movements both with and without the ball.

4. **Tactical capacity:** effective resolution to problems and speed of thought.

5. **Strategic capacity:** elaboration of previously arranged plans (foresight).

6. **Competitive capacity:** to perceive, analyse and take decisions on real game situations against the opposition.

7. **Psychological capacity:** self control, concentration, motivation and leadership.

8. **Social capacity:** environment, relationships with teammates and external pressure.

9. **Capacity to adapt and incorporate new skills.**

10. **Talent.**

11. **Experience.**

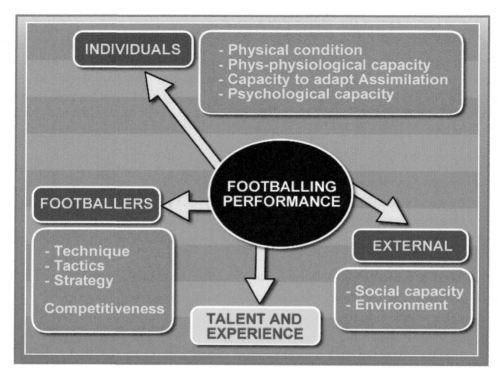

Factors that influence the footballing performance of a player (Moreno, J. 2008)

At grassroots level, these performance factors are also measurements of a young player's progress.

The tasks should be based on all aspects of football without inhibiting talent and increasing game awareness and experience. The coach for the beginning stages controls the individual factors to improve and develop, and should pay attention to external factors (parents/family) who carry a lot of influence at early ages.

In beginner's football, apart from the performance factors, we have to develop the "feeling" for:

- **The ball** - having it and recovering it.
- **The team** - to cooperate and collaborate.
- **The goal** - in search of the opposing goal.

THE METHODOLOGY OF FOOTBALL TRAINING

"The game is what teaches you, the coach/trainer guides, corrects and motivates".

The coach must be an educator and example to the player who can lead and teach. It is not only the players that are different from each other but the coaches too and this is why each team is unique.

"Order and discipline are introduced by the coach- talent and the freedom of the game are brought by the player".

The task- to lead the young player along the path, helping them to learn. Good communication between the coach and the player are vital and can mould behavior and the ability to adapt during training. Good communication is based on you speaking to the players correctly, your body language and intonation….which are all aimed at correcting and encouraging improvement. This communication should be used to direct and provide instruction, such as corrections or to provide guidance so that they do as you ask.

"Teaching through questions makes the student think, examine, judge, look and evaluate. Traditional teaching methods do not stimulate any of those processes. They encourage passivity, the very thing that coaches need to avoid". (Horst Wein)

The way to make sure they *"save"* what you are teaching could be through the use of questions, *"How could you have done that better?"*, *"What did you do wrong?"*. These help the student develop different mental solutions to enhance initiative. You can also present other problems for them to help solve.

You hear, you forget, you see, you remember, you do and you understand. A child retains between 5-10% of what a coach says. If it is discussed with an explanation and demonstration the child retains 50% and if you explain, demonstrate and guide the child through it they will retain up to 80% of the information.

Guided discovery and problem solving are very appropriate methodologies to use in football training. These methodologies help to promote autonomy and initiative in the young player, so that they think, solve and act in their own way. Knowing how and when becomes a central aspect to both solution and execution and can be corrected by the coach.

"Results mark the continuity of the coach. In training, the continuity of the coach determines the results". (Dimattia,W.)

We can create a methodological code for the learning process of the young footballer.

- The basis of the learning process is continuity and progression.
- Encourage initiative, autonomy and creativity in the young player.
- Make them understand an action before making them repeat it (recording). Teach the game based on their comprehension, first by understanding and later executing.
- Create tasks and activities and achievable challenges.
- Learn through playing and correct them at the appropriate time without interrupting the game.
- The exercise guide should not be the training model.
- Go from the top to bottom of the tasks, explaining how they should be and respecting the rules.
- Teach the technical fundamentals in tactical environments and open tasks, introducing technical-tactical links for both comprehensive and specific tasks.
- The coach/trainer should adapt the drills and tasks to the different stages and phases of training as well as to the characteristics and potential of the team.
- There are other sports that can be incorporated and used as alternative methods of teaching and training in football.

What to do?

Evaluate and control the training and the competition. The objective is to identify things that can be improved upon such as errors, strengths and weaknesses so that you can later adapt and integrate these aspects, both with individuals and the team to plan the weekly program.

How to do it?

With analytical details (aided decision making), drawn from the analysis of each player both during training and competitive games with passive opposition.

With global methodology to learn, correct, improve and mechanize the abilities of the young players, integrating technical and tactical aspects into the training tasks, progressing towards active or real opposition.

During initiation and basic football, we have to awaken the player's ability and ingenuity. Technical execution work should be progressive and gradually integrate opposition. We should always remember that football is played against opposition.

The opposition should progress from passive and inactive situations of superiority to real opposition in situations of equality.

The 2 main stakeholders in the team should comply with certain roles to ensure a pleasant coexistence:

Role of the coach/trainer

- Fewer lessons and more action.
- Make the footballer continually think.
- Explain and demonstrate.
- Ask questions in order to teach.
- Organise the relationship between space, the footballer and equipment.
- Don't cut short the tasks, let them play.
- Use the appropriate language, body language and intonation.
- Positive reinforcement, self confidence and self esteem.
- Small challenges for small achievements.

Role of the young footballer

- To understand the training objectives and the game of football.
- Good behaviour, attitude and respect.
- Order and discipline.
- Play with initiative, freedom and autonomy.
- Collective ideas, collaborate and cooperative play.

"Football is a state of mind".

In football, you depend on the state of mind to train and compete. The more confidence and motivation that you have, the better you will be capable of both doing and creating. Motivation should be the tool that the coach uses to push young players to develop all of their potential. You want them to not only compete but also to train and improve.

Emotions control behaviour and it is the obligation of the coach to manage and control these moods to benefit the collective emotional state. Anxiety and stress must be eliminated so that the youngster's emotional stability will help the training process and allow the player to improve.

There are vital points that must be enhanced every day, such as attention, concentration, sportsmanship, respect, teamwork and sacrifice for a job well done. Above all you should include a daily motivation. Cohesion in the group is key and the search for collective objectives above the individual is key in beginner's football.

"Overcoming challenges and adversity, above results and classifications".

The coach must emphasize that hard, well done work is the achievement and that achievement does not require results to achieve confidence and motivation. This is achieved by recognising and strengthening the will and effort, with more positive reinforcement and less blame and meaningless punishment. *"Words and reason speak, error and ignorance shout".*

The coach should speak and discuss things with a coherent tone and not vent their anger after a mistake. Know that any comment from a coach will affect a young player's psychological development and personality.

"There should be neither punishments nor prizes in football training, only consequences to the work being performed".

The small positive details help to construct players and should be controlled. A good method is to make small things important.

We should implant the sporting values of both football and fair play and encourage their use. Motivate so that the young players become hooked on the game and enjoy it.

Training should be all about fun and enjoyment.

Psychological criteria for the coach:

- Know the players individually and collectively.
- Guide success and downplay failure, training them to overcome adversity.
- Motivate by showing optimism, conviction and energy.
- Listen and communicate closely and coherently.
- Resolve conflicts fairly. Be fair in disciplinary decisions, respecting each team members individuality.
- Show confidence and trust.
- Create a team, enhancing the relationships in the changing room.
- Provide stimulating and accessible goals.

Remember that you do not need to hurry the technical/tactical training and that we need to influence the quality and efficiency of the actions. Good guidance at the right moment can enhance the learning of each action.

We can organize the methodology of the technical/tactical training in a simple way as follows:

1. **Analytical work** - ideally working in rows, circuits and squares using decision making and having many participants. The most important aspect is learning.

2. **Technical games** - Piggy in the middle/keep-ball and possession (with 2 balls, alternative equipment etc) to adapt the movement and decision making processes during a game.

3. **Games that apply to football** - possession, movement, games, mini games with the objective of correctly executing a specific technical skill to master them (to perfect and mechanise).

4. **Matches** - more specific tasks and modified games where the techniques can be integrated efficiently into the game to perfect and mechanise.

Basic training contains aspects that are indispensable and both the order and the time spent performing them should be respected (the warm up, the main body of training and the cool down). During these periods, monitor and address the complementary aspects such as flexibility, correct hydration etc. These are all important aspects.

As for aspects surrounding the training, keep to schedules, ensure correct clothing is worn, arrive for training prepared, use the time on the field, look after the equipment, respect the changing rooms and the surroundings. All of these things are additional values that should be instilled into the young player and form part of their education.

In summary, the training methodology is based on good planning and the design of technical/tactical training tasks worked on progressively. Both full size and smaller games should be played. Create tasks that use alternates such as goalposts, playing with 2 balls and superior or equal opposition.

Change the rules from being able to play freely to 1 touch football. Increase the execution speed for concrete actions. Play with the rules of punctuation to guide the execution techniques and make them work. Above all you need to analyse and correct the decision and execution process in a sense that benefits the entire group, pointing out the right time and correct positioning for each technical action.

PLANNING FOOTBALL TRAINING SESSIONS

"Training is not the same as competing"

Competition has some determining factors that modify performance factors. Therefore, the training should contain tasks that are as close as possible to actions that occur in real competitive games, without forgetting that the goal is the progressive evolution of young football players who will form the future.

For this progression and evolution to take effect we must create a work structure based on planning that addresses the various stages and phases. Competition shows us what we need to practice, and from that we should adapt the planning to help improve the young players learning process.

Feedback, analysis and evaluation of both training and competitive matches helps to reassess and apply the relevant training. This enables us to enhance the technical and tactical performance.

Technical/tactical planning is based on both general football concepts and the specific concepts of each club team and this allows the training content to be established and developed for each footballer with respect to both their biological and chronological age.

Medium / Long Term Planning of Content				8-9 yrs	10-11 yrs	12-13 yrs	14-15 yrs	Youth
TECHNICAL	BASIC	Games	Control, shooting, tackling, finishing	1	2	3	4	
		Individual Offence	Control, dribbling, shooting	1	2	3	4	
		Individual Defence	Tackling, marking, harassment			1	2	3
		Support	Volleys, Scissor kicks, chips and lobs		1	2	3	4
		Drills	Basics, principals, technical and tactical		1	2	3	4
	SPECIFIC	Collective	Controlled passes, walls, cross field balls		1	2	3	4
		Finishing	Shooting, assists, crosses	1	2	3	4	4
		Motor functions, Physical	Coordination, running technique	1	2	3	4	
	COMPETITIVE	Systems	Movement/circulation, passing the ball out of the area, attacking			1	2	3
TACTICAL	BASIC	Games	Multiple goals, decision making games		1	2	3	4
		Possession	Keep-ball, peripheral vision, support	1	2	2	3	4
		Matches using small goals	4 players, 6 players, indoors, outdoors		1	2	3	4
		Defensive principals	Covering, marking , off side			1	2	3
		Offensive principals	Walls, creating space, support		1	2	3	4
	SPECIFIC	Finishing	1v0, 1v1, 2v1, …10v10	1	1	2	3	4
		Attacking	Around the area, transition			1	2	3
		Short game	Quick shots, crossing, lay offs		1	2	3	4
		Restricted game	Combinations, counter attacking, direct play		1	2	3	4
	COMPETITIVE	Dangerous situations	Defensive transition, reorganizing attack			1	2	3
		Stable situations	Set pieces			1	2	3

1. Learn 2. Intergate 3. Master 4. Automate

When in the planning stages, we should be mindful of the different stages of training to best suit the needs of the young footballer.

Phases of Technical-Tactical Training

		Objectives	Methods	Opposition	Stages (Ages)
1	Analytical	Learning technical resources in decision making situations	Lines, individual tasks	No opposition	10-11 yrs 12-13 yrs
2	Technical Games	Adapting and dominating technical gestures in decision making situations	Box drills, circuits, adapted games	Passive/ active	10-13 yrs 14-15 yrs
3	Team Drills /Possession	Assimilation and integration of the resources and game tasks	Oriented possession Inferiority Equality Superiority	Modified active	10-11 yrs 12-13 yrs 14-15 yrs 16-17-18 yrs
4	Games that apply to football	Execution of gestures used in real game situations	Game application Reduced games	Specific high	12-13 yrs 14-15 yrs 16-17-18 yrs
5	Specific applications- lines and systems	Consolidation and optimization of the technical resources available to the group	Line applications Finishing Modified matches	Specific maximum	14-15 yrs 16-17-18 yrs
6	Matches	Maximum efficiency and use of resources in real game situations.	Transitions Game applications in reduced real situations	Maximum competitive	14-15 yrs 16-17-18 yrs

To respect the methodological progression, you can create training routines that address each of the phases of formative football.

There should be a long term plan although daily improvements will lead to a need for constant modification as both the players and the team learn.

The classification of the methods falls into 3 large groups:

Routine Basic Session for 10-11 year olds

	1st Session		2nd Session		3rd Session	
Preliminary Session	Proprioception	5	Proprioception	5		
Warm up	Joint mobility	1	Joint mobility	1	Joint mobility	1
	Game (basic)	3	Game (at speed)	3	Individual technique - offensive	7
	Team drills – keeping possession- basic	5	Team drills-keeping possession- basic	5	Game suggested by the group	6
	Motor skills and technique (Running technique and agility)	8	Motor skills circuit and relays. (Coordination and balance)	8	Individual technique- defensive	7
Main body	Individual technique (offensive and defensive)	20	Collective technique	15	Set pieces	15
	Possession, keeping and progressing		Finishing	20	Attacking resources	15
	Basic tactics 1v0, 1v1,2v1, 2v2, 3v2	25	Short game	15	Match	20
	Small Sided Game Breadth/depth 4-6-8 players		Restricted games			
Cool down	Individual technique	6	Individual technique/game	6	Freestyle or foot volleyball	10
	Relaxation and chatting	4	Relaxation and chatting	4		

Routine Basic Session for 12-13 year olds

	1st Session		2nd Session		3rd Session	
Preliminary Session	Preventive routine	5	Preventive routine	5		
Warm up	Joint mobility	1	Joint mobility	1	Joint mobility	1
	Team drills – keeping possession-basic	4	Team drills-keeping possession-basic	4	Team drills-keeping possession-specific	4
	Game (basic)	3	Game (at speed)	3	Game (at speed)	3
	Motor skills and technique	10	Motor skills circuit	6	Coordination, agility, fast paced	8
Main body	Individual technique	15	Collective technique	15	Set pieces	12
	Possession		Finishing	20	Finishing	15
	Basic tactics	30	Restricted games	20	Pre-Game	25
	Small Sided Games		Short games			
Cool down	Individual technique	4	Individual technique	4	Individual technique	4
	Flexibility routine	4	Flexibility routine	4	Flexibility routine	4

Routine Basic Session for 14-15 year olds

	1st Session		2nd Session		3rd Session	
Preliminary Session	Preventive routine	5	Compensation routine	5	Preventive routine	
Warm up	Joint mobility	1	Joint mobility	1	Joint mobility	
	Team drills – keeping possession-Basic	4	Team drills-keeping possession-Specific	4	Team drills-keeping possession-Competitive	
	Game (basic)	3	Game (at speed)	3	Game (at speed)	
	Motor skills and technique	10	Motor skills circuit	6	Coordination, agility, fast paced	
Main body	Physical circuit	15	Individual & team technique	10	Set pieces	
	Individual & team technique	12	Finishing	15	Finishing	
	Possession		Attacking Possession	15	Pre-Game	
	Basic tactics	20	Restricted game			
			Short game	20		
	Small Sided Games		Restricted matches			
Cool down	Individual technique	4	Individual technique	4	Individual technique	
	Flexibility routine	4	Flexibility routine	4	Flexibility routine	

Routine Basic Session for 16-17-18 year olds

	1st Session		2nd Session		3rd Session	
Preliminary Session	Preventive routine	8	Compensation routine Gymnasium	25	Preventive routine	8
Warm up	Joint mobility	1	Joint mobility	1	Joint mobility	1
	Team drills – keeping possession-Basic	4	Team drills-keeping possession-Specific	6	Team drills-keeping possession-Competitive	6
	Game (basic)	3	Game (at speed)	3	Game (at speed)	3
	Motor skills and running technique	10	Running technique Explosiveness	10	Coordination, agility, fast paced, reaction times	10
Main body	Physical circuit	15	Team technique	10	Finishing	15
	Individual & team technique	15	Finishing	10	Pre-Game	45
	Possession		Restricted game			
	Specific tactics	30	Short game	30		
	Small Sided Games		Restricted matches			
Cool down	Individual technique	5	Individual technique	5	Individual technique	5
	Flexibility routine	5	Flexibility routine	5	Flexibility routine	5

Methods for Technical-Tactical Training

General	Motor coordination qualities	Individual	Group	Team	Set pieces
Basic	Warm up Rows Circuits Box drills/diamonds	General analytical With decision making	Possession drills Combined actions	Games Exercises and finishing	Analytical
Specific	Circuits Combined actions	Comprehensive analytical with decision making. Positions Lines	Applicable games Oriented possession	Restricted/short games Application Lines Competitive situations	Restricted games
Competitive	Attacking Combined actions	Specific analytical with decision making Differentiation	Attacking Application Lines	System application Restricted real situations Matches	Matches

The classification of the methods falls into 3 large groups:

1. **Basic** (general elements)
2. **Specific** (specific elements)
3. **Competitive** (elements specific to competitive situations)

These are subdivided into individual, group and team.

Example of General Technical / Tactical Training for: 10-11 year olds

1. Learn / 2. Intergate	Pre season		MACRO-CYCLE 1		MACRO-CYCLE 2
OBJECTIVES	Learn both individual and collective execution mechanisms		Learn and integrate specific execution mechanisms. Enhance and expand the resources		Improve and master the specific execution mechanisms
General methods	Basic	Specific	Competitive	Specific (S)	Competitive
Analytical/resources	1 1 1 1 2 2			1 1 2 2	2
Technical game	1 1 1		2 2	1 2 1 2	1 2 2
Possession drills	1 1	1 1	1 1 1 1	2 2	2 2 2 2
Possession	1 1	1 1	1 1 1 1 1	2 2	2 2 2 2
Small Sided Games	1	1 1 1 1 1 1 1 1 1 1 1 1		2 2	2 2 2 2 2 2
Finishing		1 1 1 1 1 2 1 2 1 2 1 2		2 2	2 2 2 2 2 2
Application games		1 1 1	2 2 2 2		2 2 2
Match	1 1 1		1 1 1 1	2 2 2 2	2 2 2 2

THE SESSION IN FOOTBALL TRAINING

"The session is the minimal unit of programming required for daily improvement".

We arrive at the daily sessions and the training. Improvement is a result of good work day after day, adapting to the different circumstances that arise during every training session without losing sight of the overall and planned objectives.

A good way of reaffirming the work done in a session could be to repeat the session twice with the same objectives in order to remember and improve what was practiced, increasing the assimilation capacity of the desired objectives.

The variety of training, drills and exercises should be enjoyable for the young footballer. You can design different sessions to emphasise the skills you are working on, without setting aside or forgetting the desired results.

A casual way to have fun that highlights the work achieved could be to organise a "football day". Once every 3 to 4 weeks a whole session could be aimed at improving and using the fundamental skills learned during the previous sessions. For example: Dribbling day, shooting day, marking day, set pieces day.

These sessions can be organised around the drills that the young players enjoy the most.

Technical/Tactical Circuit Warm-Up   20 min

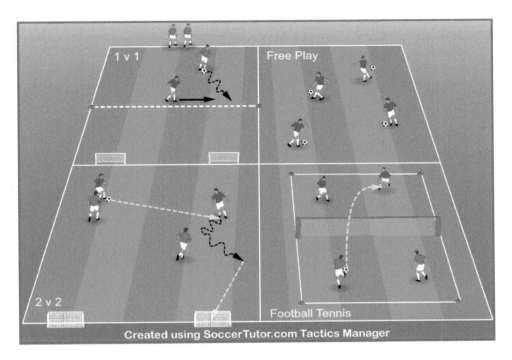

Objective
For the players to warm up with free play or with technical aspects integrated into situations with competitive opposition. 5 minutes per section. Rotate players.

Description
Section 1 - Players aim to dribble the ball past their opponent in a 1 v 1 Duel.

Section 2 - Free play where players practice technical ground or juggling skills.

Section 3 - The players play 2 v 2, with both teams defending 2 mini goals.

Section 4 - We again have 2 v 2 as the players compete in a football tennis match.

Coaching Points
Section 1 - Get the players to try different moves/feints to beat the defender.

Section 2 - Coach can give specific juggling sequences or ground moves/feints.

Section 3 - Quick accurate passing and creating space key to scoring goals.

Section 4 - Play 1 bounce or no bounce depending on ability or age of players.

Possession and Finishing Small Sided Game

15 min

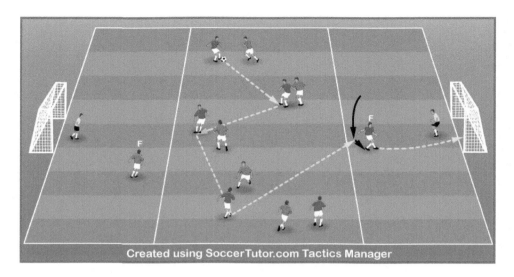

Created using SoccerTutor.com Tactics Manager

Objective

To develop both attacking and defensive team play. We practice passing, receiving, pressing, crossing, marking and shooting techniques.

Description

Using half a full size pitch, we play 7 v 7 with the aim of passing the ball to the forward in the end zone to score a goal. Inside the middle zone play with unlimited touches.

When the forwards are passed the ball they use a maximum of 2 touches to score past the goalkeeper.

Coaching Points

1. Teach players to angle their body in relation to where the defender is, always protecting the ball.
2. Drag your marker away to create space for others.
3. You need awareness and communication to move the ball quickly to the forward.
4. Encourage players to look up to spot that decisive pass as early as possible.

Crossing and Finishing Small Sided Game

20 min

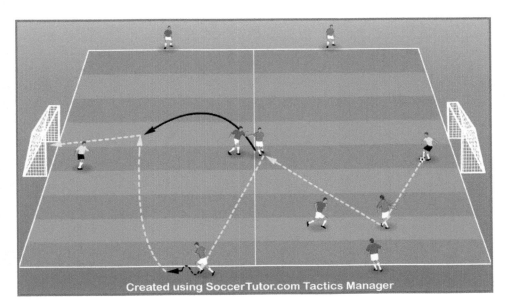

Created using SoccerTutor.com Tactics Manager

Objective
To develop fast attacks, crossing and finishing.

Description
Using an area double the size of the penalty area we play 2 v 2 within the square. Each team has 2 outside players with 1 in the defensive half and the other in the attacking half.

The players play with 2 touches and the aim is to pass the ball to the wide player in the attacking half who crosses it for the players inside to run onto and finish with either a volley or a header.

Coaching Points
1. Play and think quickly.
2. Running into space to receive the ball to fully exploit numerical advantage.
3. The cross needs to be well timed for the oncoming run.
4. The team in possession really need to attack the crosses, timing their runs well.

Triangular Support Play in a Small Sided Game

20 min

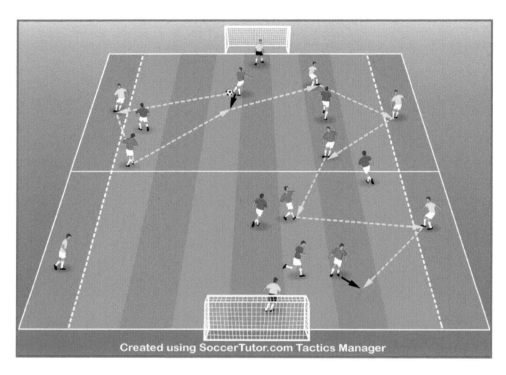

Objective
To develop possession and support play.

Description
Using a quarter of a full pitch we play 5 v 5 with 5 extra utility players.

The players play with 2 touches within the area and the utility players play with 1 touch. Any shots or headers on goal should also be with 1 touch.

Coaching Points
1. Triangular support: when a player receives the ball there should be an option to the left and right of them.

2. Create space and lose the marker to fully exploit the numerical advantage.

3. Encourage players to receive the ball half turned and receive and pass with the back foot.

Warm Down: Headers and Tackles Game

5 min

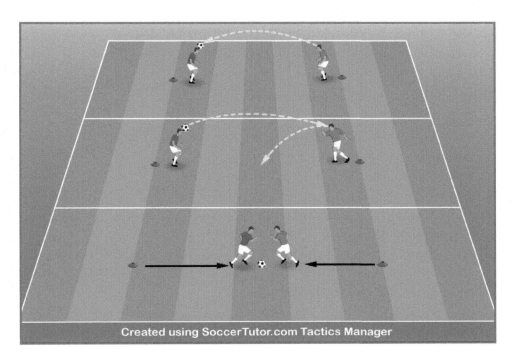

Created using SoccerTutor.com Tactics Manager

Objective
To warm down while improving heading ability and quick reactions (50/50 tackles).

Description
The players are in pairs and head the ball to each other at a distance relative to their ability or age.

When 1 player fails to head the ball back to their partner and it falls to the ground, both players aim to retrieve the ball quickly. When 1 player gains possession of the ball the other player attempts to tackle them.

Coaching Points
1. Headers should be high allowing the partner time to return the ball more easily.
2. When the ball drops, quick acceleration is needed to get there first.
3. When 1 player retrieves the ball, their aim is to use their body to protect it.

CHARACTERISTICS OF TRAINING

- It has to stimulate intelligence, autonomy and creativity.
- It should be varied to encourage the ability to adapt.
- It should be motivating so that the player enjoys it.
- Have simple rules and explain them clearly.
- Follow the routines and the order of the exercises.
- Progressively integrate the drills and exercises.
- Be dynamic and continuous without stoppages.
- Make the practices demanding but flexible.
- The drills should be specific and comprehensive.
- Ensure there is a good warm up with proper hydration and a cool down ending with flexibility (stretches).
- 2 way communication (dialogue with questions and answers to get feedback).

What not to do!

- Difficult exercises or ones designed for or copied from adults.
- Explanations without demonstrations.
- Very intense exercises or continuous running.
- 2 consecutive sessions with the same objectives to remember and improve.

THE TASKS IN FOOTBALL TRAINING

The analysis of maximum efficiency in football should begin when planning the training tasks.

The achievement begins when we avoid being beaten and batter the opponent's goal.

When designing the tasks you should adapt them to the level of the youngsters and take into account any variables to increase the ability of the players to assimilate and adapt. The ability to provide different solutions to the given situations is also key.

Guidelines

- Different and varied tasks without prejudice to the objective, using exercises that motivate and meet the objectives to increase ability.
- Give multiple solutions to increase the responsiveness to different situations.
- Do not limit the training with excessive rules and be facilitators, not regulators.
- Integrate the opposition as much as the football, but always gradually starting from a passive position and later becoming more active and real.
- Create technical/tactical games based on the essence of football.
- Create corrective games and exercises, to improve any shortcomings and errors discovered through the analysis of both the training and the competition.

To ensure that the technical/tactical tasks are progressive, we can organize them in a simple and accessible way such as:

- **Games or possession:** 1 v 0, 1 v 1, 2 v 1, 3 v 2, 2 v 2 to work on attacking and defensive principals, both individually and as a group.
- **Decision making drills:** technical work with attacking and defensive principals using decision making skills, selecting runs, marking and covering.
- **Superiority possession:** (4 v 2 – 12 v 6) improve the attacking principals with switching play, escaping the marker, changes of position.
- **Inferiority possession:** (2 v 6 – 6 v 12) improve defensive principals (marking, covering, interceptions).
- **Restricted games:** matches played with a number of players and space to improve any collective attacking or defensive action (pressure, switching play, marking lines, support).
- **Application games:** matches with a technical and tactical orientation in real game situations.

PRACTICAL ASPECTS OF TECHNICAL/TACTICAL TRAINING IN GRASSROOTS FOOTBALL

"Training is putting the planning into action".

The coach should continually adapt to what happens during training in order to help the young player assimilate and improve on a daily basis.

Beginning training requires organisation, attention to the players, a peripheral vision so that no details are missed and the ability to combine all of these so that the training is focused on the desired objectives.

Practical aspects of training

- Take a plan with you to training and put a copy up in the dressing room so that the player can begin to understand the aims of the session.
- Explain the session prior to starting, highlighting the desired objectives.
- Keep to schedules and exercise times.
- Take notice of the kit and personal appearance of all team members.
- Have all equipment available, in good condition and organised.
- Don't waste time during training, gain it (give out bibs before it starts, have 2 drills prepared, do not wait for rotations, do not stop to correct).
- The training should always be well structured and have ample time for warm up, the main body of training and a warm down.
- Respect the hydration and stretching periods (each player should have a bottle of water).
- The coach must be responsible for respect and education, taking care with their words and the way they speak to the young player and ensure they use an appropriate tone.
- Encourage the use of both feet, the head (both attacking and defensive aspects).
- Ensure that motor responses, coordination and speed prevail over strength.
- Perform speed work through games, relays and circuits.

- Be careful with the circular possession drills, ensure fairness and show the players how to be both independent and team players.
- Be careful with punishments because reinforcement teaches more than 5 punishments does.
- Collect up all of the equipment together forming group cohesion and continuous collaboration.
- Keep explanations and demonstrations simple, with the "whys" and "what for's".
- The coach should be the first person to arrive and the last to leave. Finish tired from encouraging, strengthening and teaching.

A session aimed at the improvement of technical/tactical aspects should be progressive from beginning to end. It should begin with a general analysis and finish as specific and competitive. This should be from more to less in terms of participation, from the most simple to the most complicated and from confined spaces to larger open spaces.

Ball Control, Agility and Speed Warm-Up

15 min

Created using SoccerTutor.com Tactics Manager

Objective

To develop coordination, agility and speed training and technical ball control.

Description

Use half a full size pitch. Rectangle in middle should be 40 x 30 yards. With almost every player having a ball there is a large participation.

Group 1

Practice ball control, speed, agility, and coordination.

- 1st set of cones - dribble with 1 foot, inside 1 touch and then outside 1 touch.
- Pass the ball beyond the ladder, run through it (left then right foot) before retrieving the ball again.
- 2nd set of cones - the same as the 1st with the other foot this time.
- Pass the ball beyond the speed rings, hop one leg at a time (left, then right) through them and then retrieve ball on other side and return to the start.

Group 2

- The 4 players within the square practice dribbling, turning and moves/feints.
- The outside players without the ball play 1 touch passes back to the players within the square when they are passed the ball by them.
- The outside players can also be used as inactive or active defenders within the square.

Make sure to rotate all the players so everyone gets an equal chance for all aspects of the exercise.

Ball Control and Awareness Warm Up

10 min

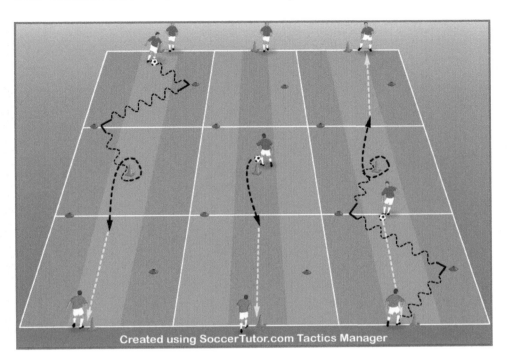

Created using SoccerTutor.com Tactics Manager

Objective
To develop ball control, escaping markers, passing and awareness.

Description
The 3 sections are 10 yards in length each.

In the 1st section dribble outside, then cut back inside. In the 2nd section players dribble to the cone and turn 360° around it before passing to the player waiting in section 3 who performs the same sequence from the other side.

Coaching Points
1. This exercise requires quick and sharp movement to keep it dynamic.
2. Stress the importance of these movements to escape a marker in a game.
3. In the 1st section, exaggerate the sharp change of direction.
4. All players should keep the ball close to their feet.

Aerial Passing & Finishing Small Sided Game

15 min

Created using SoccerTutor.com Tactics Manager

Objective

To develop fast attacks and practice technical skills - aerial passing, crossing and volleying/heading.

Description

Use an area double the size of the penalty area. Add an extra ball after 5 minutes.

This is a technical finishing game, so players should try to score goals with headers, volleys or scissor kicks from wide crosses. Only heading may be used to intercept the ball. All passes should be volleys or headers. Start with unlimited touches.

Coaching Points

1. Play and think quickly.
2. Running into space to receive the ball to fully exploit the numerical advantage.
3. Monitor the correct technique for lofted passes.
4. The team in possession really need to attack the crosses, timing their run well.

Possession Game: 5 v 5 (+ 5)   15 min

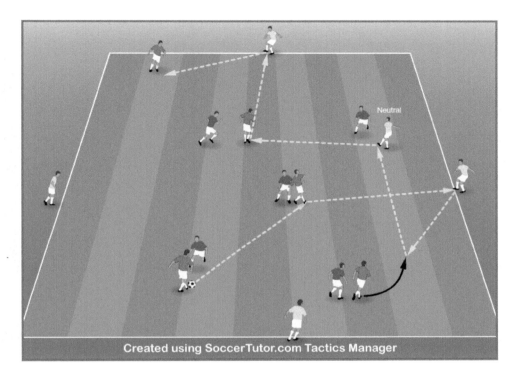

Created using SoccerTutor.com Tactics Manager

Objective
To develop passing, possession and creating space (unmarking).

Description
Using 1 or 2 balls we play 5 v 5 with 5 extra utility players. All players play with 1 touch.

This is a competitive game. Encourage good play with a successful dummy or 10 consecutive passes winning a point. If the ball goes out of play it is a throw-in. If a player loses the ball they leave the square for a set period of time.

Coaching Points
1. Using 1 touch makes the need to get away from your marker and move into space key to success.
2. The players need to be constantly moving to fully exploit the numerical advantage and maintain possession.
3. The defenders must press together and have good cohesion to retrieve the ball.

Collective Technical Training Exercise

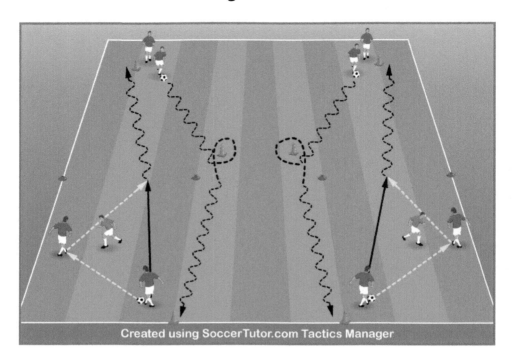

Created using SoccerTutor.com Tactics Manager

Objective

To develop dribbling, ball control, short passes and 2 v 1 duels.

Description

Using half a full pitch we play with 2 balls. All players work at the same time.

In sections 1 and 2 there are 2 v 1 duels. The players must get past the defender and the ball carrier goes through the cones and dribbles to points 3 and 4 respectively.

Sections 3 and 4 are playing at the same time. They both dribble towards the cone and turn 360° around it before dribbling towards positions 1 and 2 respectively.

Coaching Points

1. The players use both feet and all parts of the foot.
2. The intensity and speed of the exercise needs to be high.
3. Movements with the ball should be sharp replicating movements away from defenders.

Quick Pass, Move and Decision Making in a SSG   15 min

Objective
To develop passing, receiving, pressing, movement after passing/driving forward.

Description
Using half a full pitch we play a 6 v 6 game with 3 teams.

This is a cognitive exercise to train decision making. There are 2 rules the players must follow - they must change positions with their teammate after their pass and can only use 1 touch if they receive the ball from a teammate after advancing forward. The team that gets a goal keeps playing. The other team is replaced by the 3rd team waiting at the side.

Coaching Points
1. Encourage quick and sharp movements to create fast attacks.
2. Using only 1 touch the body position is key, protecting the ball from the defender.
3. Defenders need to not simply be attracted to the ball, making sure to be mindful of the space in behind.

Passing and Possession 5 v 2 Warm Down

10 min

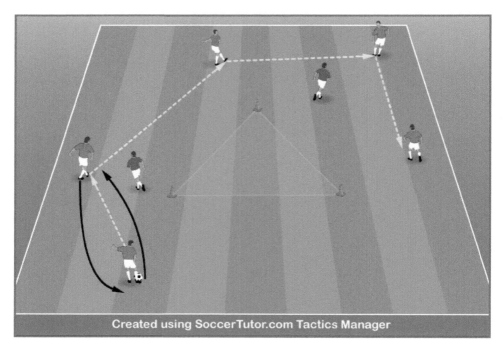

Created using SoccerTutor.com Tactics Manager

Objective
To develop passing, possession and player movement.

Description
A triangle is positioned on the centre of the area.

Play 5 v 2 with team in possession not allowed to move or pass through the triangle.

Coaching Points
1. Good body shape to be aware of the next pass and to receive
2. The players need maintain a good body shape even whilst moving into space.

STREET FOOTBALL

"I learnt in Arguíneguin, playing with other kids in the street", (David Silva)

One thing that the youngsters do not have so much these days is the possibility of playing football in the street. Society has changed the customs, values and priorities of the youth. The football schools that were the thousands of miles of streets are in decline.

"Football in the school yard is a form of teaching".

Football played in the square, on recreation grounds or on the beach is a form of football without tactical binds, systems and fixed positions. Everyone attacks and everyone defends.

In football friendships are made through getting to know your teammates over the course of a game. This is a game where 1 against 1 is an exciting duel and a situation that everyone wants and looks for, where inventing a new trick is met with "oooohs" and "aaahs", and later everyone tries to copy and imitate.

Football without rules? In street football the essence of football is at its purest. The decisions that are taken are essential for the understanding of the game. They cover their teammate who is trying to steal the ball, they defend individually and collectively against the best player, they play zonal marking when they are tired, they run to take a shot and play more cautiously when against a better defence.

They make many decisions that form the basis for club training where they can improve and perfect their game.

And the duels? We have all looked to beat that person that we know is better than us, or maybe even the best. It is purely for the satisfaction, to win this challenge or individual battle.

And what about the little grudges between classes or friendly groups playing in the street? Healthy grudges are what make any match. When pride is at stake the game is worth the most, and pride in a collective sense can create cooperation and stronger team values than can ever be given to them by a club. These *"street"* values also help mould the young player's personality.

These games do not need referees but the game and the rules are respected, creating an autonomous personality and providing both the individual and the group with sporting values which are difficult to achieve through training. If there is a foul the game stops, if the ball goes out of play the game stops. What it is, it is, full stop. If in doubt, there is a discussion, but the discussion always ends with a compromise, one for you and one for me if the issue was not resolved through discussion. The rules of the game are learnt and discussed, all of which helps the youngster to learn.

The laws of the game are unchangeable although the rules may change from street to street, for example when you let in a goal, you touch the crossbar for the next player to get between the sticks so that everyone defends and is close to the goal. It is more collective, there is more solidarity and there is more communication and more association.

And how about the allocation of different roles, not positions? There will always be a *"leader"* who tells the others where to play. Organisation is achieved with a relational base that few teachers are able to achieve. This communication and discussion to reach an agreement develops the social and relationship skills of the child, which should always be taken into account.

This football broadens relationship aspects, strengthens friendships and creates broad ties that last through time. Decision making skills are increased through playing pure football, as well as autonomous organisational skills and both the team and individuals personality, but most of all it makes "football" football and nothing else, where enjoyment is the most important thing and everyone gives it their all, and if someone does not, there will be someone who remembers that next time!

During training the recommendation would be that once in a while play matches where there are no established rules. Just 2 teams, two goals and the space that you want, playing the rules that they want and refereeing them, provoking, generating and favouring all that was explained above.

CONCLUSION

Training should care for, respect and strengthen talent and the innate abilities of the young prospective footballers, taking into account that we should also classify, plan and train them to become that.

We have to take care of the training from the grassroots level, encouraging creativity and decision making abilities in the young players during a game, but also motivate them and help them enjoy playing.

We need to ultimately promote sporting and personal values that guarantee their development, as much in football as personally and educationally.

BIBLIOGRAPHY

- Bergier J. Buraczewski, T. "Analysis of successful scoring situations in football matches". P-137 Journal of Sports Science and Medicine (2007) Suppl. 10, page 205.

- Casajús, JA; Arjol, JL. "Exigencias físicas del futbol". Real Federación Española de Futbol. Medical services. Madrid. Spain. 2005

- Forriol Campo,F. "Análisis de los gestos técnicos específicos, superficies de juego y equipamiento en futbol". Notes from a master in physical preparation in football. RFEFUCLM- AEPFF Madrid 2006

- Garganta, J. "Hacia una formación inteligente en el futbol base". II International conference of grassroots football, City of Cartagena.

- Jones, P.D.; James, N.; Mallalieu, S.D "Possession as a performance indicator in soccer". International journal of Performance Analysis in Sport, Volume 4, Number 1, August 2004, pp 98-102 (5).

- Moreno, M. Técnica aplicada al alto rendimiento, level 3 course. RFEF National school.

- Portugal, M.A. "Medio de entrenamiento con balón en futbol, metodología y aplicación practica". Editorial Gymnos.

- Riera Riera, J. "Bases generales para el análisis funcional de la táctica deportiva". Module 1.2. Notes from a master in high performance sports. Olympic Centre of Higher Education. Madrid 2007-2009

- Seirul'lo, P. "Reflexiones sobre una nueva línea de entrenamiento". Abfutbol magazine;no 19, January 2006.

- Vales Vazquez, A. "Modelos tácticos y preparación física en futbol". Notes from a master in physical preparation in football. RFEF-UCLM-AEPFF Madrid 2006.

- Vegas Haro, G. "Creación de situaciones de enseñanza aprendizaje en futbol". XXII Conference football school updates, Seville 2003. Andalusian Football Federation.

CHAPTER 2

SANTIAGO ESPOSITO

Atlético Madrid U11
Academy Coach

ATLÉTICO MADRID U11 ACADEMY COACH PROFILE

Santiago Esposito
Atlético Madrid U11 Academy Coach

- National football coach (Level III)
- Masters in sports psychology

In this chapter there are exercises designed to improve the technical level for 8-12 year olds. There are 35 drills to help coaches work and improve various technical attributes for young football players.

There are exercises for both individual exercises and technical practices incorporating team play.

We work to improve dribbling, touch, ball control, feints, moves to beat, passing and shooting. These are practices for young players and we must always emphasise that they perfect their technique on both feet equally.

Throughout all of the exercises the young players must perform while constantly moving and using a movement forwards when receiving the ball.

During the dribbling exercises you must guide the young players so that they have the ball under very close control, looking with their head up at the space around them and not at the ball.

Their should be a big encouragement to improve their ability to manoeuvre the ball in various ways in different situations. In the dribbling exercises, the players should be encouraged to be daring and creative.

The practices should progress from having an opponent playing passively to one that becomes more active and challenging once different dribbling skills have been learnt and strengthened.

The passing practices include passes in all 3 directions: horizontal, vertical and diagonal. During these exercises we must encourage the players to communicate with each other and make accurate passes fundamentally using the inside of the foot.

The passing distances should increase as the players master the skills in accordance with the objectives of the session.

The shooting exercises should always be performed with both feet and from distances appropriate to the development of the players. When shooting, encourage the players to have good posture at the moment they strike the ball and to be coordinated throughout the action, paying more attention to the direction rather than the strength of the shot.

Within the 35 drills there are some that combine various actions (dribbling, pressing, passing, shooting etc). All of the drills should be performed with both feet so players develop a good command of the ball in all possible positions and angles.

The last 2 training exercises are more realistic game actions: one of possession and the other a "duel". In them, the players can put into practice all of the skills learnt from the previous 33 drills in a single, more comprehensive exercise.

The speed of play and size of the playing area can change depending on the technical level of the players.

The playing areas should not be too large and the duration of each drill will also depend on the age of the players. Make sure that the length of the practice is appropriate and effective for the players. Your own coaching instincts are the best for judgement here.

All of the proposed drills are subject to modifications so you can adapt them to the players and training requirements.

Technical Dribbling Warm Up

15 min

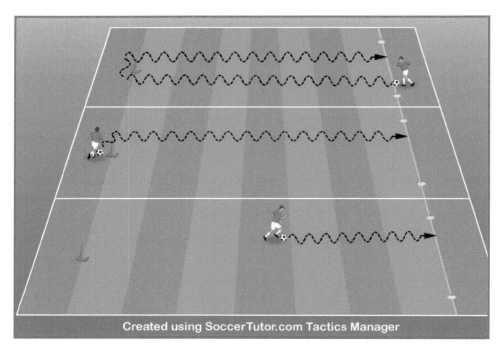

Objective
To improve dribbling technique and ball control.

Description
Players line up behind cones which are 15 yards away.

They dribble to the cone using only the right foot and after going round the cone they dribble back with only their left foot.

Coaching Points
1. Use different dribbling techniques.
2. Make sure the players use all different parts of the feet to dribble - laces, inside, outside, sole.

Ball Control and Accurate Passing

15 min

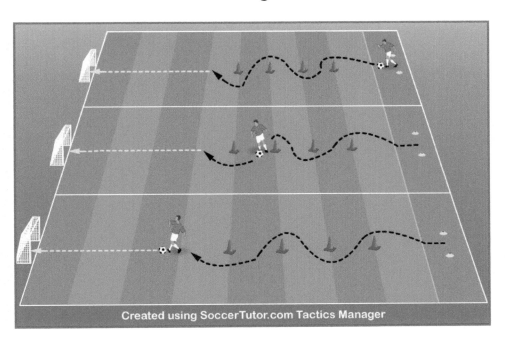

Created using SoccerTutor.com Tactics Manager

Objective
To improve ball control and accuracy of passing.

Description
Players line up behind the series of cones. The players need to dribble the ball through the cones and then pass the ball into the mini-goals, which are 15 yards away from the starting point.

Make sure the players are performing both the dribbling and the passing with both feet during the exercise.

Coaching Points
1. It is necessary to have close control of the ball through the cones, slightly bending the knees and using a balance of soft touches and speed.
2. The players should dribble the ball through the cones by using their feet alternatively (right foot and then the left foot).

Dribbling with Quick Change of Direction

10 min

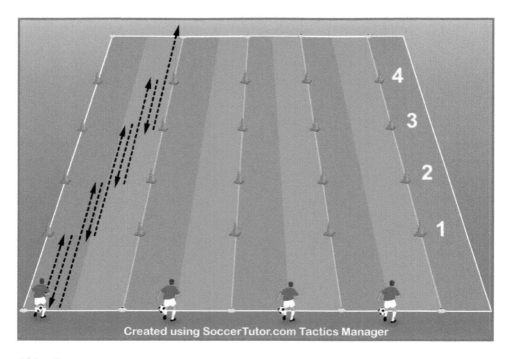

Created using SoccerTutor.com Tactics Manager

Objective

To develop the technique of ball control and running with the ball using quick changes of direction.

Description

The cones are 5 yards apart for this dribbling relay.

Players dribble to the first cone where they step on the ball and dribble back to the start.

The same sequence is repeated for the second, third and fourth cones.

Coaching Points

1. The players use both feet and all parts of the foot.
2. The intensity and speed should be high.
3. The turns should be sharp replicating a movement away from a defender.

Ball Control - Dribbling, Feints and Turning   10 min

Objective
To practice different dribbling techniques, feints, moves and changes of direction.

Description
Half of the players form a circle without the ball. The size of the circle can vary depending on the age/ability of the players.

The other half of the players dribble within the circle, making sure to avoid each other, while practicing moves and turns with the emphasis on changing direction at pace.

When the coach says 'pass' the players in the inside pass to the players on the outside and change positions with them, as shown in the second diagram.

Coaching Points
1. Make sure the players use both feet for all aspects of the drill.
2. The players need to try many different types of dribbling techniques and feints/moves outlined by the coach.
3. The turns should again be sharp replicating a movement away from a defender.
4. Accuracy and pace of pass is important and should arrive directly at the receiving player's feet.
5. Make sure the players communicate with their teammates and heads are up.

Progression
Introduce defenders into the practice - active or inactive depending on the level of the players.

Dribbling and Turning Techniques

15 min

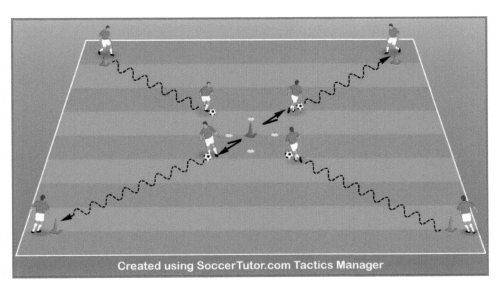

Created using SoccerTutor.com Tactics Manager

Objective
To improve dribbling technique with both feet.

Description
Using a 20 x 20 yard area, a player from each corner dribbles with one foot to the cone in the centre. Once there, they step on the ball and return to their original cone dribbling back with only the other foot.

Coaching Points
1. Make sure the players use both feet.
2. The players need to dribble with their head up, never looking at the ball.
3. The players need to be aware of the other players dribbling to the middle cone, making sure to avoid them.
4. Make sure the players use all different parts of the feet to dribble - laces, inside, outside and sole.
5. The ball should be kept as close to the feet as possible at all times during the exercise.

Dribbling with Peripheral Vision

15 min

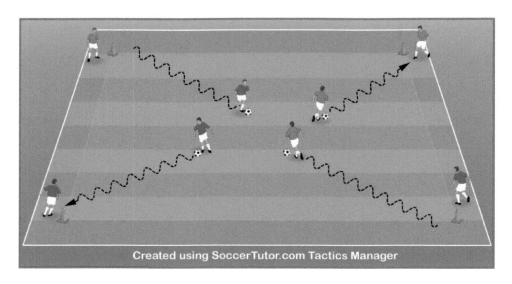

Objective
To improve awareness/peripheral vision while dribbling the ball.

Description
Using a 20 x 20 yard area, a player from each corner dribbles to the opposite corner. When they reach the opposite cone, they give the ball to the player waiting at that cone.

Coaching Points
1. The players need to use soft touches to keep close control of the ball.
2. All players heads should be up (not looking at the ball) so they are aware enough to prevent colliding with their teammates.
3. Both feet, all parts of the foot & different moves/feints need to be used to quickly move away from the other players.
4. This exercise should be started slowly, increasing the speed as the players become more comfortable.

Dribbling and Passing Techniques   15 min

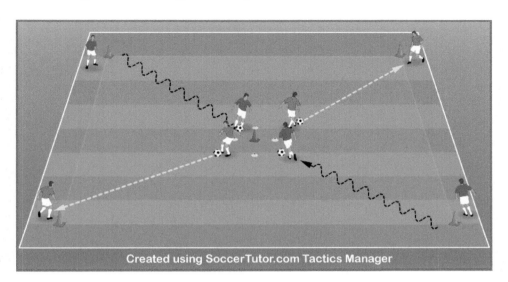

Created using SoccerTutor.com Tactics Manager

Objective
To develop ball control and passing technique/accuracy.

Description
Using a 20 x 20 yard area, a player from each corner dribbles to the cone in the centre.

When they reach the centre they step on the ball and turn back towards their original cone. The player must then pass to their teammate who follows the same sequence After passing, the first player returns to the cone in the corner to receive the next pass from their teammate.

Coaching Points
1. The players need to use soft touches to keep close control of the ball.
2. All players heads should be up (not looking at the ball).
3. The turn should be quick and sharp with the ball staying very close.
4. The pass must be accurate. It should also be correctly weighted, to allow the player to control the ball while moving forwards.

Dribbling and Passing on the Move

15 min

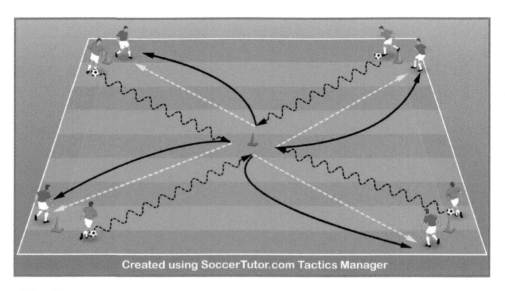

Created using SoccerTutor.com Tactics Manager

Objective
To improve ball control and passing on the move.

Description
Using a 20 x 20 yard area, one player from each corner dribbles to the cone in the centre using only the left or right foot. When they reach the centre they pass with the same foot to the player on the cone to the right of them.

The player then follows their pass to take up the position on that cone.

Coaching Points
1. The players need to use soft touches to keep close control of the ball.
2. All players heads should be up (not looking at the ball).
3. Players should utilise the outside and inside of the foot to make an accurate pass with the varied angles.
4. The pass must be accurate. It should also be correctly weighted, to allow the player to control the ball while moving forwards.

Technical Ability in Squares

15 min

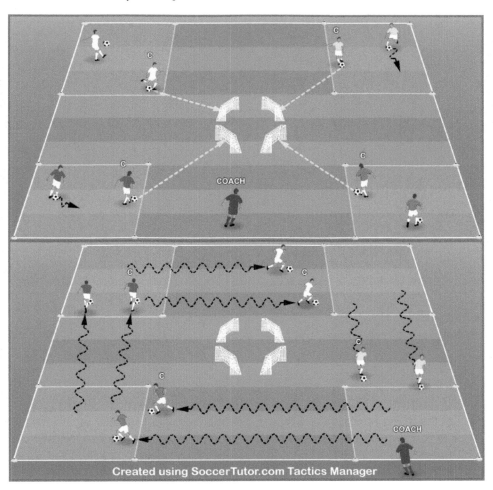

Created using SoccerTutor.com Tactics Manager

Objective
To develop ball control and accurate passing/shooting.

Description
Using a 20 x 20 yard area, 4 teams of 2 or more players, each with a captain, practice skills within their four squares.

On the whistle the captain must try to score in their assigned mini goal in the centre.

At the signal "change" all the players dribble the ball to the next square. The team that arrives in the box first with both players with the balls at their feet wins a point.

Coaching Points
1. Constantly change the dribbling method.
2. Constantly change the captain so each player gets to practice their striking accuracy.

Individual Ball Control and Finishing 'M'

20 min

Created using SoccerTutor.com Tactics Manager

Objective

To develop ball control and shooting/finishing.

Description

A player from each side sets off and dribbles the ball in and out of the boundary poles.

When they arrive at the next part of the exercise, they go around the set of poles as shown.

Finally, the player must dribble past the defender and shoot on goal before reaching the 2 coaching poles in the centre. After 10 minutes swap the players to the other side so they play with both feet.

Coaching Points

1. The players need to try many different types of dribbling techniques and feints/moves outlined by the coach.
2. The defender can be active or inactive depending on the level of the players.
3. Changes of direction through the poles should be sharp with a drop of the shoulder.
4. The tempo should be quick with players using both feet in all parts.
5. Change the defenders to give everyone an equal chance at all parts of the exercise.

Feinting and Finishing Passageway (1)

20 min

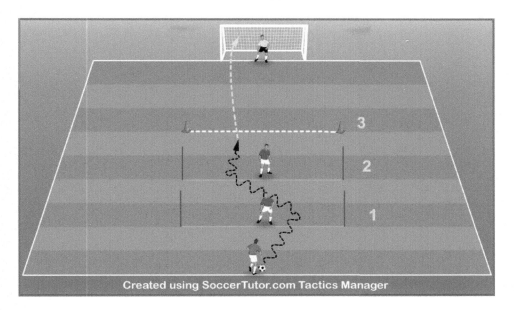

Created using SoccerTutor.com Tactics Manager

Objective
To practice feints/moves and the technique of shooting.

Description
There should be a space of 15 yards in between each of the 3 stages.

The player with the ball sets off dribbling the ball while performing feints and various moves to overcome 2 defenders situated between the coaching poles. If they get past both defenders they must shoot before they reach the line between the cones.

Coaching Points
1. Start with the defenders being inactive, then half active and finishing with fully active.
2. Change the defenders frequently.
3. Practice various types of shot - laces, inside and outside of the foot.
4. Progress the players from running up slowly to shooting at a full sprint.

Feinting and Finishing Passageway (2)

20 min

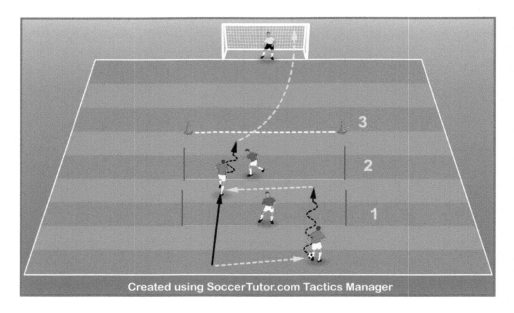

Created using SoccerTutor.com Tactics Manager

Objective

To practice playing in a 2 v 1 situation and shooting at goal (finishing).

Description

There should be a space of 15 yards in between the 3 stages.

In pairs the players use various techniques such as dribbling, passing and feints to advance past the defenders situated between the coaching poles. If they get past the 2 defenders they must shoot before reaching the line between the cones and without being offside as they pass the last defender.

Coaching Points

1. Remove the offside stipulation for younger players.
2. Dribble the ball close to the feet so the pass can be played early.
3. Timing of the runs needs to be coordinated to the pass.
4. Encourage one-two combinations and make sure they are quick and sharp.
5. Change the defenders frequently.

1 v 1 Duel: 'Who will end up as number 1?' 20 min

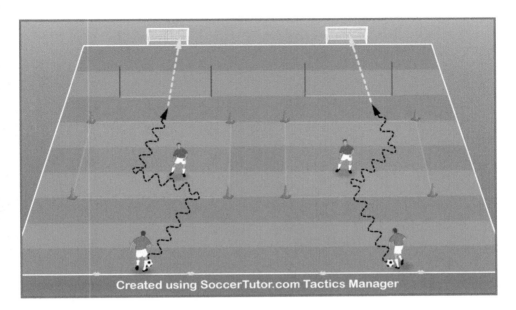

Created using SoccerTutor.com Tactics Manager

Objective
To improve moves/feints and the accuracy of passing on the move.

Description
Use an area 30 yards in length. Each player dribbles the ball to get past the player in the box using feints and various moves specified by the coach.

Once past the defender and before reaching the 2 coaching poles the player shoots into the mini goal.

Coaching Points
1. Perform the drill with various players to maintain pace and intensity.
2. Have the players set off at the same time, so that they can compete - the first one to score gains a point.
3. The attacking player needs to keep the ball close to their feet using feints and quick changes of direction to get past the defender and score.
4. Again, change the defenders so that everyone gets to participate.

Diagonal and Vertical Passing Drill

10 min

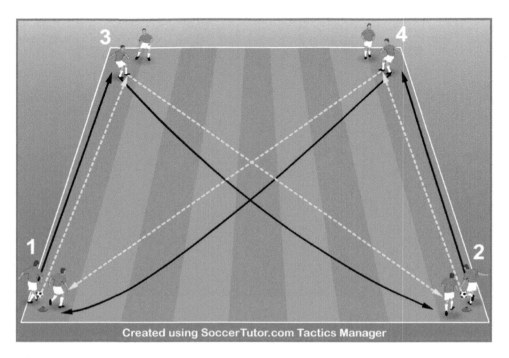

Objective
To improve cross field (diagonal) and down the line (vertical) passing.

Description
The cones should be 10-15 yards apart. From points 1 and 2 the players pass vertically to points 3 and 4 respectively. When 3 and 4 receive the ball they pass diagonally across the box to points 2 and 1.

After passing, all players run to the point where they have passed the ball to.

Coaching Points
1. Improve the speed of play by limiting the players to 1 touch when possible.
2. Change the direction of the drill to make sure all players use both feet.
3. Make sure the players communicate with their teammates and heads are up.

Progression
1. You can add 2 more balls (4 in total) depending on the number and the ability of the players.

Diagonal and Lateral Passing Drill

10 min

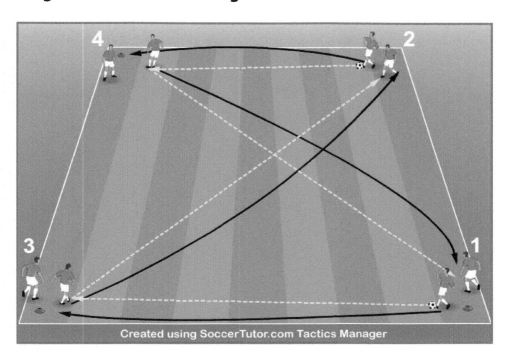

Created using SoccerTutor.com Tactics Manager

Objective
Improve the cross field ball (diagonal) and the lateral (horizontal).

Description
The cones should be 10-15 yards apart. From points 1 and 2 the players pass horizontally to points 3 and 4 respectively. When 3 and 4 receive the ball they pass diagonally to points 2 and 1.

After passing, all players run to the point where they have passed the ball to.

Coaching Points
1. The correct body shape should be monitored (opening up) and receiving the ball with the back foot (foot furthest away from the ball).
2. Improve the speed of play by limiting the players to 1 touch when possible.
3. Make sure the players communicate with their teammates and heads are up.

Progression
1. You can add 2 more balls (4 in total) depending on the number and the ability of the players.

Vertical, Diagonal and Horizontal Passing Drill

10 min

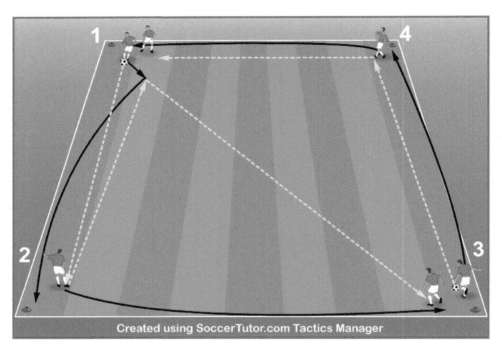

Objective
To practice vertical, diagonal and horizontal passing.

Description
The cones should be 10-15 yards apart. From points 1 and 3 the players pass vertically at the same time to points 2 and 4 respectively. When the player at point 2 receives the ball he passes it back to point 1. Then player 1 passes it diagonally to point 3.

When the player at point 4 receives the ball he passes it laterally (horizontally) to point 1. After passing, player 1 moves to 2 after the second pass, 2 to 3, 3 to 4 and 4 to 1.

Coaching Points
1. Move to meet the ball and approach it half-turned in positions 1, 3 and 4.
2. The correct body shape should be monitored (opening up) and receiving the ball with the back foot (foot furthest away from the ball).
3. Change the direction of the drill so that the players pass and receive with both feet.

Passing 'Y' Shape (1) - Give & Go with Dribble   20 min

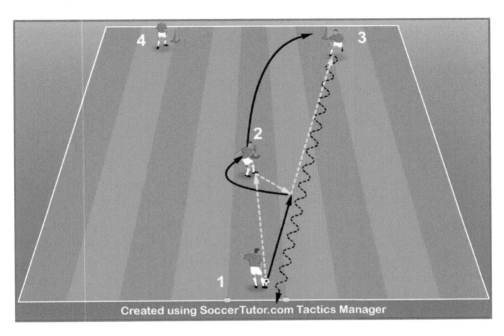

Objective
To develop short and medium range passing as well as dribbling.

Description
Cone 2 should be 8 yards away from Cone 1. Cones 3 and 4 should be 20-30 yards away from cone 2.

The players line up in a 'Y' shape. Player 1 passes to player 2 who returns it to 1.

Player 1 then passes to number 3.

The movement of the players is as shown on the diagrams.

Player 3 controls the ball and dribbles quickly to position 1. The next sequence starts from position 1 but towards the other side of the 'Y' as shown in the 2nd diagram.

Coaching Points
1. The second pass (lay-off) needs to be weighted well for player 1 to receive the ball on the move, who should time their run for the pass.
2. Make sure players pass and receive with both feet.
3. Progress the practice by limiting the players to 1 touch.
4. Make sure the players communicate with their teammates and heads are up.

Passing 'Y' Shape (2) - Give & Go with Dribble   20 min

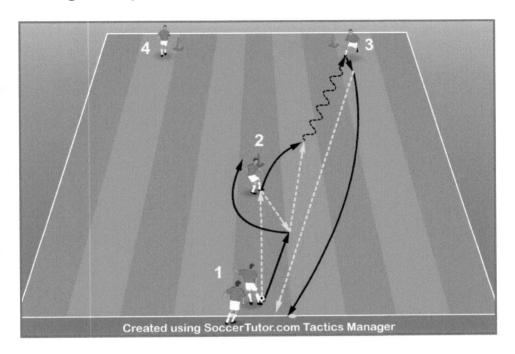

Created using SoccerTutor.com Tactics Manager

Objective
To develop short and medium range passing.

Description
Cone 2 should be 8 yards away from Cone 1. Cones 3 and 4 should be 20-30 yards away from cone 2.

With the players positioned in a 'Y', player 1 passes to player 2 who passes the ball back to player 1, who then returns it again to 2. Player 2 controls it to dribble quickly to player 3, who then controls the ball and plays a long pass back to player 1.

The movement of the players is as shown on the diagrams. Player 1 moves to position 2 when the final pass is made. Player 3 moves to position 1 and starts the sequence again to the left this time.

Coaching Points
1. After player 2 lays of the pass to player 1, his run should be well timed so the pass is in front of him.
2. In some cases, player 2 may need to hold his run and also arch his run to create the space for the player 1 return pass.

Passing 'Y' Shape (3) with Combination and Dribble

20 min

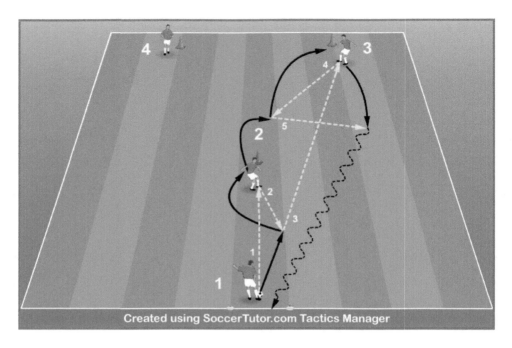

Created using SoccerTutor.com Tactics Manager

Objective
Improves short and medium range passing.

Description
Cone 2 should be 8 yards away from Cone 1. Cones 3 and 4 should be 20-30 yards away from cone 2.

With the players positioned in a 'Y', player 1 passes to player 2 who returns it to 1 so that 1 can pass first time to player 3 who combines with player 2 and subsequently dribbles the ball to position 1. They then start again playing to the left side.

Coaching Points
1. Reduce the time between the first touch and the pass, and then progress to 1 touch when possible.
2. Passes in the combinations need to be weighted well and aimed in front of the teammate so they can run onto the ball.
3. The passing and dribbling should be done at a high tempo.

2 Touch - Receive, Pass and Follow

20 min

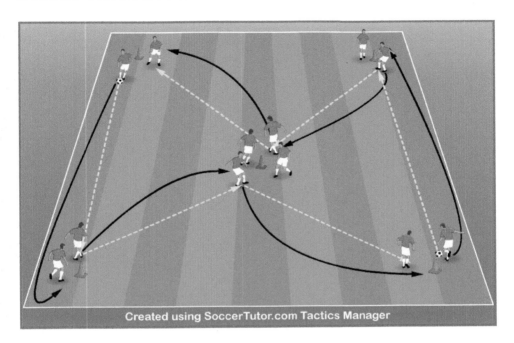

Created using SoccerTutor.com Tactics Manager

Objective
To improve receiving and passing at different angles.

Description
In an area of 20 x 20 yards with 2 or 3 players around each corner cone, the players make vertical and diagonal passes that should be controlled so that a pass can be played to the next cone.

Each player should follow their pass to take up the position at the next cone. Start with the ball at 2 cones diagonal to each other.

After 10 minutes change the direction so that the players use both feet.

Coaching Points
1. Players need to move to meet the ball and open up their body ready to receive.
2. The players need to make sure their first touch is made on the move to maintain the fluency of this drill.
3. Make sure the players communicate with their teammates and heads are up.

One-Two Triangle Passing Combinations

20 min

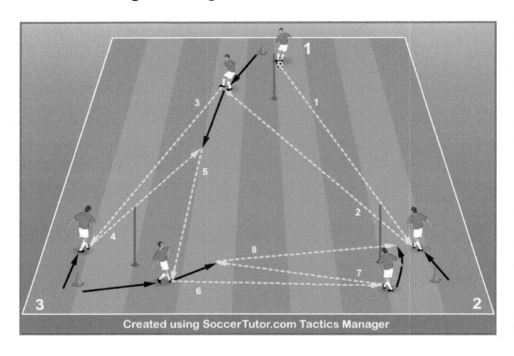

Created using SoccerTutor.com Tactics Manager

Objective

Improves short passing and timing of movement.

Description

In a triangle with the cones 20 yards apart there are 2 or 3 players per cone. They set off dribbling from 1 and 3 towards 2 and 1 respectively. The player with the ball passes to the next player in the sequence as shown in the diagram.

The passes played in front of the coaching poles need the player who receives it to control it whilst running. After 10 minutes change direction so the players have to use both feet.

Coaching Points

1. Players should move to meet the ball to increase the speed of play.
2. Open body shape - half turned and receive/pass with the back foot.
3. Runs need to be timed well when creating space and should be done at pace.
4. Make sure the players communicate with their teammates and heads are up.

2 Touch Diamond Passing Drill

10 min

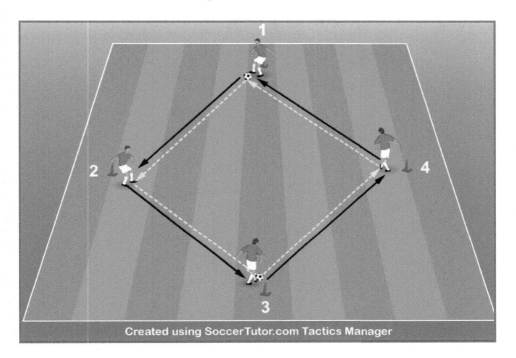

Created using SoccerTutor.com Tactics Manager

Objective
To improve control and diagonal passing.

Description
With the cones at a distance of 10-15 yards from each other, the players make diagonal passes to the next cone so that the receiving player can control the ball and make a diagonal pass to the next cone.

After making the pass the player goes to the cone he passed the ball to. Play with 2 balls that start at points 1 and 3.

Coaching Points
1. Players should move to meet the ball to increase the speed of play.
2. At this angle the players should have the correct body to shape to allow the ball to run across their body to receive and pass with the back foot.

Progression
Introduce 4 balls depending on the number and ability of the players.

Continuous Shooting

10 min

Created using SoccerTutor.com Tactics Manager

Objective
To improve shooting technique while dribbling with the ball.

Description
The goals should be about 30 yards apart with the coaching poles in the middle. Line the players up next to the goals with the 2 groups diagonal to each other.

The players dribble to the side of the coaching pole in the centre and shoot at the goal. After 5 minutes move the players to the other goal post.

Coaching Points
1. Players need to keep the ball close to their feet using both the left and right.
2. Place the other foot next to the ball when striking. The head should be over the ball and the player should strike straight through the ball.
3. Body shape needs to be straight and angled towards where the shot is aimed.
4. Use different parts of the foot to shoot - laces, inside and outside.

Continuous Shooting with Pass

10 min

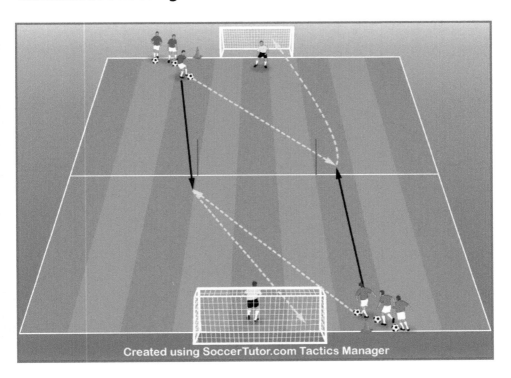

Created using SoccerTutor.com Tactics Manager

Objective

To improve technique of shooting after an angled pass.

Description

The goals should be about 30 yards apart with the coaching poles in the middle. Line the players up next to the goals with the 2 groups diagonal to each other.

A player, after making his pass, runs without the ball to the coaching pole in the centre, receives a pass from the opposite side and shoots at goal.

Coaching Points

1. The pass and run needs to be well timed and coordinated.

2. The players should use a maximum of 1 touch to control before shooting.

3. When receiving the ball the touch needs to push the ball away from the body allowing space to strike through the middle of the ball with their head over it.

4. If possible shoot first time.

Shooting 'Y' Shape (1) - Pass with Give & Go   20 min

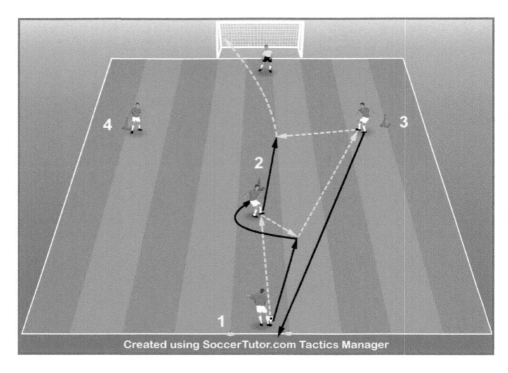

Created using SoccerTutor.com Tactics Manager

Objective
Improves short and medium range passing with shooting first time direct from a pass.

Description
Cone 2 should be 8 yards away from Cone 1. Cones 3 and 4 should be 20-30 yards away from cone 2. Position the players in a 'Y'. Player 1 passes to player 2 who returns it to player 1, who then passes to 3, who returns the ball to player 2 nearer the goal so that player 2 can shoot.

The next player leaves from position 1 but towards the other side of the Y. The movements of the players are 1 to 2, 2 to 3 (after the shot) and 3 to 1 after collecting the ball.

Coaching Points
1. Players should use short steps when running up to shoot.
2. The timing of the final run relies on the awareness and the anticipation of when player 3 will play the ball.
3. The final pass needs to be out in front of player 2 so that they can run onto the ball and strike it first time.

Shooting 'Y' Shape (2) - Pass with Give & Go   20 min

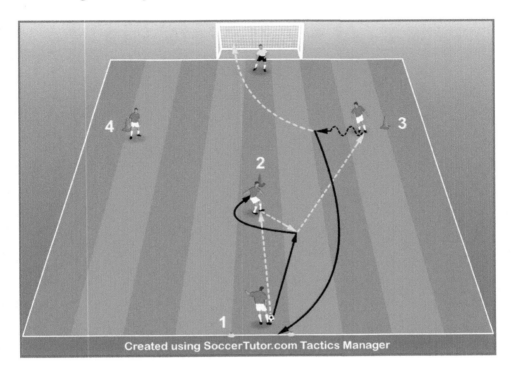

Created using SoccerTutor.com Tactics Manager

Objective
Improve short and medium range passing and shooting after receiving and moving with the ball.

Description
Cone 2 should be 8 yards away from Cone 1. Cones 3 and 4 should be 20-30 yards away from cone 2. Position the players in a 'Y'. Player 1 passes to 2 and 2 returns it to player 1 so that 1 can pass to 3. After returning the ball to 1, 2 moves to position 3 and player 1 moves to position 2.

Player 3 must control the ball inward and shoot at the goal. The next player sets off from position 1 but to the other side of the Y.

Coaching Points
1. Player 3 should receive the ball with 1 touch, play the ball out in front of the body quickly and inwards towards the goal making it easy to shoot.

Shooting Wheel (1)

20 min

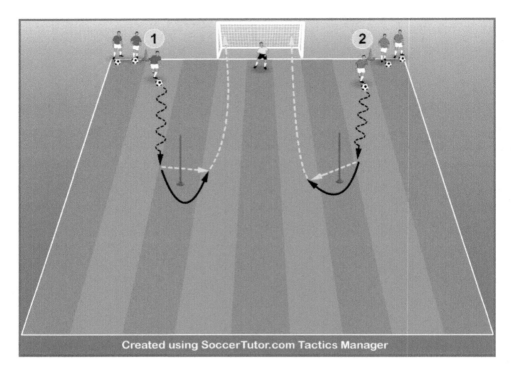

Created using SoccerTutor.com Tactics Manager

Objective
To practice shooting when running onto the ball and turning in limited space.

Description
The coaching poles should be 20 yards from the goal.

The players line up behind the cones in the corners of the goal-line. One at a time, they dribble the ball up to the coaching pole where they play the ball slightly in front of it and run round it to meet the ball.

The player then controls the ball and shoots at the goal. The players at cone 1 dribble and shoot with the right foot and the players from cone 2 dribble and shoot with their left. After 10 minutes change the players over so that they work on both feet.

Coaching Points
1. In the movement round the pole the players need to keep low to create a sharp change of direction, slowing down before accelerating towards the ball.

2. The weight of the pass to themselves needs to be coordinated with the time it takes to run around the pole.

3. Encourage the older or more developed players to shoot first time highlighting the importance of maintaining balance and getting their head over the ball when shooting.

Shooting Wheel (2)

20 min

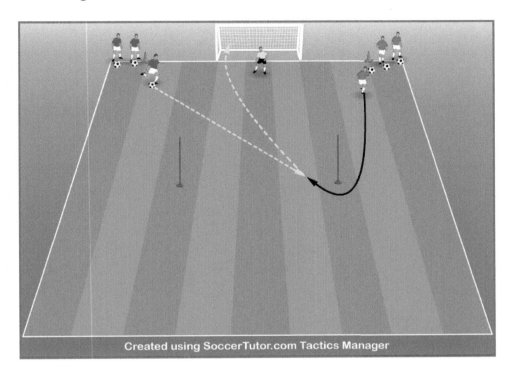

Created using SoccerTutor.com Tactics Manager

Objective
Improve shooting technique after receiving a pass.

Description
The coaching poles should be 20 yards from the goal. The players line up behind the cones in the corners. In order, they run round the pole where they receive a pass from a player at the cone on the opposite side and shoot at goal.

The players from cone 1 pass and shoot with the right foot and the players from cone 2 pass and shoot with the left. After 10 minutes change the players over so that they work with both feet.

Coaching Points
1. In the movement round the pole the players need to keep low to create a sharp change of direction, slowing down before accelerating towards the ball.

2. Encourage the older or more developed players to shoot first time highlighting the importance of maintaining balance and getting their head over the ball to shoot.

Passing and Shooting 'N' with Dribble and Movement   *20 min*

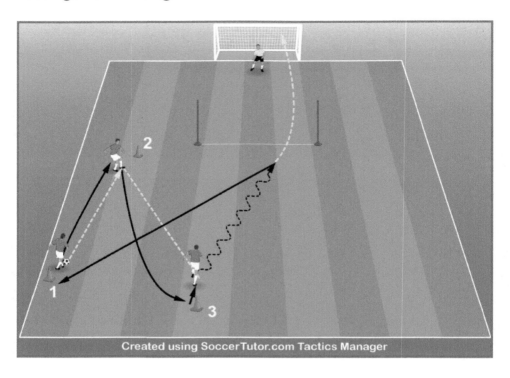

Created using SoccerTutor.com Tactics Manager

Objective

Improves short passing and shooting after a forward run.

Description

Player 1 passes to Player 2 who controls the ball and passes to player 3 who also controls the ball. Player 3 then dribbles to the coaching poles where he shoots at goal.

The movements are from 1 to 2 after passing, 2 to 3 after passing and 3 to 1 after shooting and collecting the ball. Change the drill to the other wing and repeat it with the other foot.

Coaching Points

1. Passes should be firm and accurate.
2. Whilst dribbling, player 3 needs to keep the ball close to their feet.
3. Player 3 needs to push the ball away from the body allowing at least a full stride with their head over the ball before striking it.

Symmetrical Passing and Shooting (1) 20 min

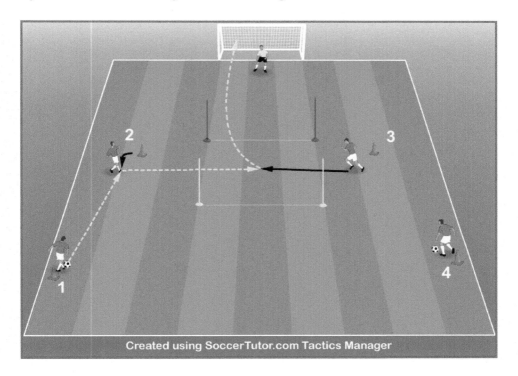

Created using SoccerTutor.com Tactics Manager

Objective
Improves short passing and receiving/shooting after a sideways pass.

Description
Player 1 passes to Player 2, 2 controls the ball and passes to 3 who runs with the ball into the shooting box outlined by the coaching poles and shoots at the goal.

After the shot, player 3 collects the ball and goes to point 1 to begin again. The movements are 1 to 2, 2 to the box, shoots and goes to 4. 4 to 3, 3 to the box, shoots and goes to 1. The sequence starts again with Player 4 passing to player 3.

Coaching Points
1. Player 3 should receive the ball with 1 touch, play the ball out in front of the body quickly and inwards towards the goal.

2. Player 2's pass needs to be nicely weighted so Player 3 can control it easily or shoot first time if progressing the exercise.

3. Player 3 should turn their body towards the goal, with their head over the ball when striking.

Symmetrical Passing and Shooting (2)

20 min

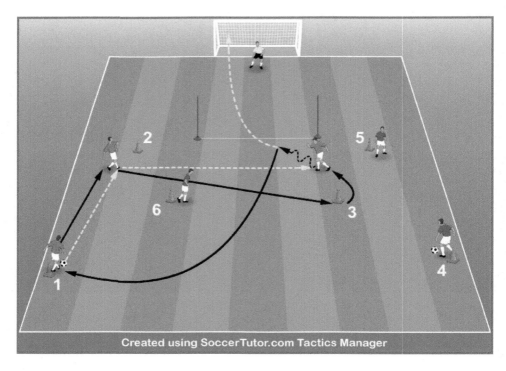

Objective
Improves short passing and shooting skills after a diagonal movement.

Description
Player 1 passes to Player 2, 2 controls the ball and passes to 3 who also controls the ball and dribbles up to the coaching poles where he takes a shot at goal with the left foot, then collects the ball and returns to position 1.

The players in positions 4, 5 and 6 then do the same from the right but 6 shoots with the right foot. After 10 minutes change the players around so that they use both feet.

Coaching Points
1. Player 2 needs to approach the pass with an open body shape in the direction of the next horizontal pass making it quicker and easier to execute.
2. Player 3 needs to time his movement well and not go too early.

1 v 1 Duels in a Small Sided Game

30 min

Created using SoccerTutor.com Tactics Manager

Objective
Improves collective movement, pressing, passing, shooting and ball control.

Description
In an area of 20 x 20 yards play 3 v 3 with both teams trying to score a quick goal.

On the coach's whistle, the players come off the field leaving the ball where it is and 2 other teams enter to continue the game with the score remaining the same.

Coaching Points
1. Encourage the players to play at a high tempo, play freely and be creative.
2. Players need to create space in the right areas to receive the ball.
3. Coach players to receive the ball on the half-turn to develop their awareness of other players' positions.
4. Players should attack the space in behind the defenders, using various feints/moves.

Technical Possession Game with 4 Corners   20 min

Created using SoccerTutor.com Tactics Manager

Objective
To develop short passing, ball control and team possession with an active opposition.

Description
We play 6 v 6 with 2 players from each team located in 2 opposite corners of a square area of play. The teams try to keep possession of the ball changing the direction from one corner diagonally to the other.

When a player passes to a player in the corner, that player must control the ball and dribble into the main play area and the player that gave him the ball takes his position in the corner (they swap).

Coaching Points
1. Passes should be fast and accurate.
2. Body shape of players should always be half-turned, aware of team-mates and the opposition.
3. When a player in the corner box receives the ball, their teammates need to make supporting angled runs to both the left and right.
4. Quick combinations are needed and passes should be made into player's paths.

CHAPTER 3

JOSE A. FERNANDEZ LOPEZ

Real Madrid U15
Academy Coach

REAL MADRID U15 ACADEMY COACH PROFILE

Jose A. Fernandez Lopez
Real Madrid U15 Academy Coach

- Formerly coached at Atlético Madrid
- National football coach (Level III)

Philosophy in the world of football has changed a lot in the last few years. It is all a lot more methodical, complex and very much more professional.

It is really everyday experiences that make a coach grow both on a personal and professional level. It is simple: you must continually take steps forward, mindful of the needs of the players that are at your disposal and through your understanding of the sport. You must be professional yet you should strive to improve and learn at all times.

A coach must encourage the game through dynamic, structured drills.

Through time and the sessions that we develop we will see improvement in the players both as individuals and collectively. For that to happen, we should remember that experience consists of constantly asking questions.

We should continuously analyse what we are doing and this will benefit our level of performance and ultimately aid the player and the team's development.

From Monday to Friday we should treat the players as people and as players on match day. We should understand each player as an individual to bring out their full potential performance. How do we mange that? Easy answer, we do this in the sessions we develop throughout the week.

We must have great capacity for observing and absorbing information. Football is a marriage of improvisation and organization and in order for the player and team to use the skills they have accumulated they must understand their role. We are obliged to set tasks during the week to make sure objectives are achieved.

An important quote to me that I was told was that **"the mind of a footballer is like a parachute, if it doesn't open it doesn't work".**

Information and guidance at the psychological level of the player and team is extremely important, exchanging information with the group as you work with them.

The player's psychological strength should be a focus, as in the end this is key for them to perform to their full potential.

We all need the necessary profile and to work naturally, not to try to copy any other coach.

Essential points for me are, without doubt, work, an ideology and good group management. All of this is right, but you can never forgive a coach if his team doesn't play. This is why the training, the daily work and the essence of the drills that we schedule is what being a coach is all about and what makes you elite or not.

In football we have to have one thing clear, in the same way that we ask our players for strength and solidarity, we must be the first people to take care of all of the details and be important TO them, not only for them. We have to encourage a sense of belonging and affection for the club, we have to take care of the kit men, work with the medical staff, with the directors, with the club's commitments, with the people that support you and the people that don't, but above all we must take care of the players.

Players should be treated warmly and a good relationship is key to coaching a team. Simple aspects such as a goodbye each day or a handshake are necessary. In the end, the players are in charge and that should always be clear.

The coaches aim should be to always have a clear conscience of a job well done.

We need to tell players over and over the things that they should hear. We should make them self-critical. We must insist that they assess their own performances and that they are the references for their own improvement, that they respect decisions and are receptive to developing aspects that need improvement.

Training is the fundamental part of the development of players. As one of my colleagues often says **"I know what I look for as I know what I feel".**

No aspect of training should be left out and we have to use all our knowledge to develop and constantly improve our training sessions. The exercises set out in this chapter are based primarily on the pursuit of basic goals in football today to produce the level that we want from our teams.

What do we want from our players?

- Commitment to the club
- Sense of belonging
- Respect for the history
- Technical excellence
- Understanding of the game and its dynamics
- Ability to solve game situations
- Ability to overcome opponents
- Dynamism
- Decisiveness
- Domination of both individual and tactical understanding
- Need own initiative
- Courage
- Solidarity and full effort
- Ability to improve and achieve
- Ambition

What do we want from our teams?

- To play freely
- Play at a high tempo
- Depth and breadth of play
- Be intense without the ball
- Disrupt the other teams balance
- Be offensive with a balanced defence
- Try to regain the ball quickly after losing it
- Try to be organised without the ball

What do we want from our coaching team?

- Active participation in the group dynamic
- Creation of work cycles
- A willing to develop and improve
- An ability to put ideas into context
- Professional work record
- Continuous reflection for individuals and the group
- Highly organised sessions
- Conduct the practice with dedication and passion
- High level of involvement in the sessions

From the drills that we are going to develop the players will obtain good control of the ball and be able to advance, combining with teammates without losing it the ball.

The players are obligated to actively participate in all of the drills and each of the variables to have a full development of all necessary actions, regardless of positions/

We always insist that the ball be the first reference of any drill, although there is no game without movement.

In collective work we must stress that the objective is not to be perfect but to encourage versatility and creativity. As we often say, **"look for variants that increase the complexity".** We should pay very close attention to detail.

The drills that we perform should always reflect actual game situations and emphasize the vital elements of the game.

Individual Technique (1) - Ball Control Warm-Up 10 min

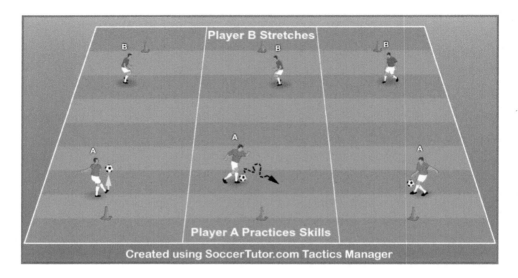

Objective
Warm up for the session while practicing various techniques.

Description
In an area of 20 x 15 yards, each pair has a ball and the players are placed 10 yards apart facing each other.

While the player with the ball practices their skills on the ground or in the air their teammate performs stretches.

Players should swap positions after 2 minutes.

Individual Technique (2) - Aerial Control

10 min

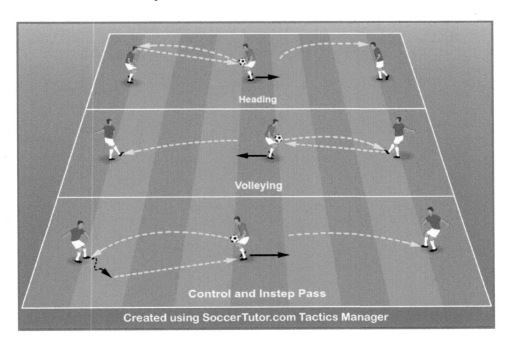

Objective
To practice aerial control and passing.

Description
Use an area of 15 x 30 yards.

In threes, one has the ball in their hands in the middle and the other two are 5 yards away, facing him. The middle man throws the ball and the other 2 execute the different actions alternately. Change the middle man to share the role.

1. High throw - head it back with the first touch.
2. Mid-range throw - volley pass.
3. Low throw - control and return it with the instep.

Coaching Points
1. The throw is very important and should be consistent.
2. Players playing the ball can start by standing still but should end the exercise moving forward towards the ball when playing it.

Individual Technique (3) - Ball Control and Passing

2-5 mins per drill

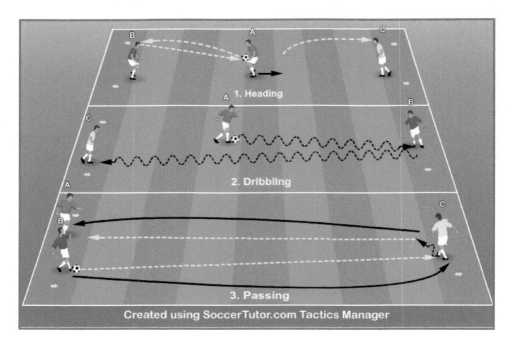

Created using SoccerTutor.com Tactics Manager

Objective
To develop heading, dribbling and passing/receiving technique.

Description
In an area of 25 x 20 yards, players are in threes with two on one side and the other 15 metres away facing them.

1. Player A is in the middle and throws the ball up for the others to head it back.
2. Player A dribbles the ball to player B where he goes around him and steps on the ball, leaving the ball to continue the relay.
3. Pass, control with one foot and return it with the other foot. After passing switch positions.

Coaching Points
1. Rotate the players' roles in the heading section.
2. The exercise should be done with high intensity with the players using full speed as each section is only 2-5 minutes long.
3. For the passing and dribbling make sure players use both feet and all parts of the foot.

Individual Technique (4) - Passing

5 mins per drill

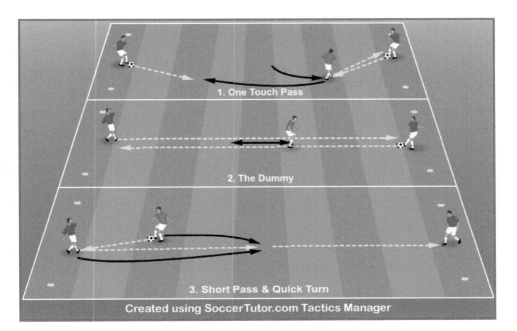

Objective
To develop passing technique.

Description
Using half a full size pitch the players are in threes, 1 placed in between the other 2.

1. The players on the outsides each have a ball. They pass it to the player in the middle alternately and returns it using 1 touch.

2. The player on the outside passes it to the player in the middle who dummies it and lets the ball run to the third player who plays it back for the player in the middle to dummy it again and let it run back to the first player.

3. The player in the middle has the ball and passes to one of the outer players who plays it round the first player for them both to chase. Whoever gets there first passes the ball to the other outer player.

Coaching Points

1. For the first section the player in the middle should receive the ball with the back foot with their body half turned to best be able to make the next pass.

2. In the second section the player needs to weight the pass very well to reach the player on the other side through the middle player.

3. In the third section the player in the middle should not turn to chase the ball until the pass has been played.

4. All sections should be played with high intensity to replicate game situations.

Passing Triangle (1) with Quick One-Two

20 min

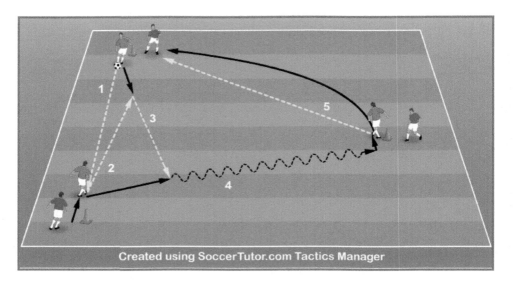

Created using SoccerTutor.com Tactics Manager

Objective

To develop passing, receiving and movements needed to create space.

Description

In a field area of 15 x 20 yards players are in groups of 6 forming a triangle.

The players receive the ball and pass it with the same foot. Players should follow their pass and take up the position at the next cone. Play the drill in the opposite direction to work both feet. Players run to the next cone after completing their final pass. Limit the players to 1 touch depending on their level.

Coaching Points

1. Create space (check) before moving to meet the ball.
2. Body shape should be open and players should use the back foot to receive/pass.
3. The timing is very important so that the ball is constantly moving.
4. As the players are performing the whole drill with 1 foot so change which one they use often.
5. Make sure the players communicate with their teammates and heads are up.

Passing Triangle (2) with Double One-Two   20 min

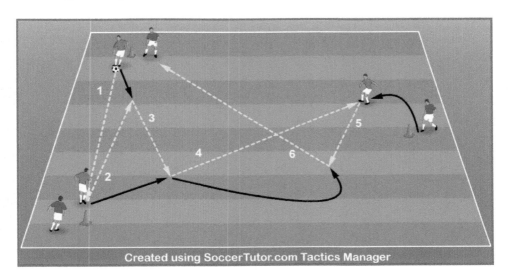

Created using SoccerTutor.com Tactics Manager

Objective
To develop passing, receiving and movements needed to create space.

Description
In a field area of 15 x 20 yards players are in groups of 6 forming a triangle.

The players receive the ball and pass it with the same foot. Players should follow their pass and take up positions at the next cone. Play the drill in the opposite direction to work both feet. Players run to the next cone after completing their final pass. Limit the players to 1 touch depending on their level.

Coaching Points
1. The correct body shape should be monitored (opening up) and receiving the ball with the back foot (furthest away from the ball).
2. Passes should be of high speed and accurate.
3. The timing of movement for checking away and moving to meet the ball is very important so that quick play is maintained.
4. Make sure the players communicate with their teammates and heads are up.
5. As the players are performing the whole drill with 1 foot, change which one they use often.

Passing Triangle (3) with Triple One-Two   20 min

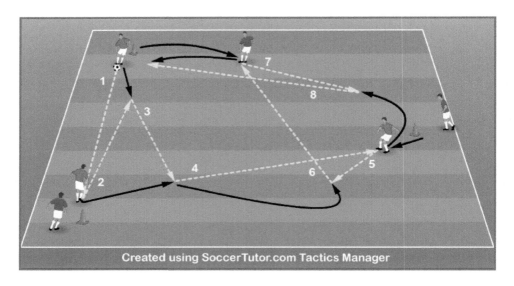

Created using SoccerTutor.com Tactics Manager

Objective
To develop passing, receiving and movements needed to create space.

Description
In a field area of 15 x 20 yards players are in groups of 6 forming a triangle.

The players make **'assist'** passes. Players should follow their pass and take up position at the next cone. Play the drill in the opposite direction to work both feet. Players run to the next cone after completing their final pass.

Coaching Points
1. The timing of the pass is key, making sure the ball is played ahead of the next player to run onto.
2. The player should check away with an open body shape before moving to receive the pass.
3. Passes should be of high speed and accurate.
4. Make sure the players communicate with their teammates and heads are up.

Passing Triangle (4) with Assists
20 min

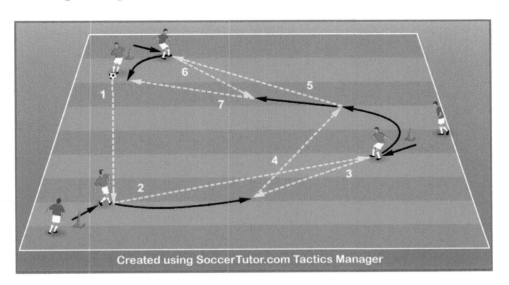

Created using SoccerTutor.com Tactics Manager

Objective
To develop passing, assists and timing of movement.

Description
In a field area of 15 x 20 yards players are in groups of 6 forming a triangle.

The players make **'assist'** passes. Players should follow their pass and take up position at the next cone. Play the drill in the opposite direction to work both feet.

Players run to the next cone after completing their final pass.

Coaching Points
1. All players should receive the ball on the move.
2. Players should time their movement well when creating space. It must be made while the pass is travelling between the 2 previous players.
3. Players receiving the assist must open their body, arch their run and time it well so the assist (i.e. pass 4) is in front.
4. Make sure the players communicate with their teammates and heads are up.

Passing Square (1) with Dribble

20 min

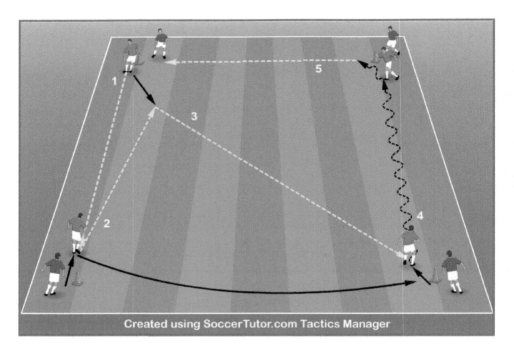

Created using SoccerTutor.com Tactics Manager

Objective
To develop passing and receiving.

Description
In a field area of 15 x 15 yards players are in groups of 8 forming a square.

Start with 1 ball and the first player passes the ball, receives a return ball and makes a diagonal pass. The next player controls it and runs with the ball to the teammate facing him who takes the ball and passes it back to the first position.

All players receive the ball on the move and control it with the same foot they pass with. Practice in both directions so that both feet are worked. Players move to the next cone after passing.

Coaching Points
1. Encourage the players to check to create space before moving to receive the ball.
2. Encourage the players to look up even when dribbling to make sure the passes and movements are accurate.
3. Make sure the players communicate with their teammates and heads are up.

Passing Square (2) with Quick One-Two and Dribble   20 min

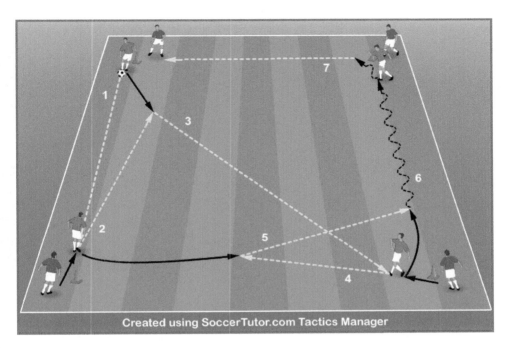

Created using SoccerTutor.com Tactics Manager

Objective
To develop passing, receiving and movements needed to create space.

Description
In a field area of 15 x 15 yards players are in groups of 8 forming a square.

Start with 1 ball and the first player passes the ball, receives a return ball and makes a diagonal pass. A one-two is played before the player controls the ball and runs with it to the teammate facing him who takes the ball and passes it back to the first position.

Practice in both directions so that both feet are worked. All players receive the ball on the move and control it with the same foot they pass with. Players move to next cone after passing.

Coaching Points
1. The timing of the pass is key, making sure the ball is played ahead of the next player to run onto.
2. The player should check away with an open body shape before moving to receive the pass.

Passing Square (3) with Short-Long Combination   20 min

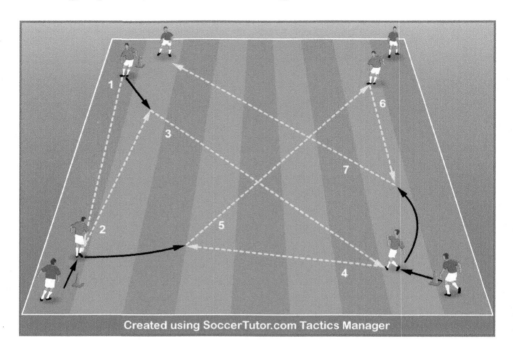

Objective
To develop passing, receiving and movements needed to create space.

Description
In a field area of 15 x 15 yards players are in groups of 8 forming a square.

Different types of support appear in this drill. This is what we call a **"short-long game"** where, after frontal support you should look for depth. Practice in both directions so that both feet are worked. Players move to next cone after their last pass.

Coaching Points
1. All players receive the ball on the move and control it with the same foot they pass with.
2. The player should check away with an open body shape before moving to receive the pass.
3. Passes should be of high speed and accurate.
4. Timing of movement in support is important. Not too early!

Passing Diamond (1) - Pass + Return + Deep Pass   20 min

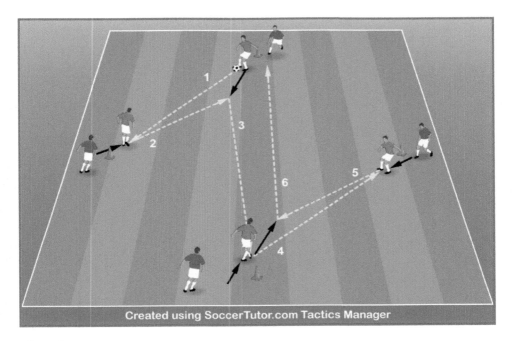

Created using SoccerTutor.com Tactics Manager

Objective

To develop passing and receiving.

Description

In a field area of 15 x 15 yards players are in groups of 8 forming a diamond shape.

Start with 1 ball, the first player passes, receives the return and plays a deep vertical pass. The next player controls and plays another one-two, before returning the ball to the starting position.

Practice in both directions so that both feet are worked. All players receive the ball on the move and control it with the same foot they pass with. Players move to the next cone.

Coaching Points

1. Create space by checking before receiving the pass.
2. At the diagonal angle the players should have the correct body shape to allow the ball to run across their body to receive and pass with the back foot.

Progression

1. You can use 2 balls depending on the number and ability of the players.
2. Progress the exercise by limiting the players to 1 touch.

Passing Diamond (2) - Pass + Control + Pass

20 min

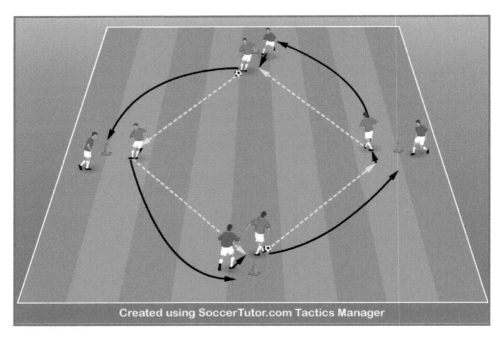

Created using SoccerTutor.com Tactics Manager

Objective
To improve passing and receiving at angles.

Description
In a field area of 15 x 15 yards players are in groups of 8 forming a diamond shape.

Start with 2 balls, the passes are all made at an angle round the diamond.

Practice in both directions so that both feet are worked. All players receive the ball on the move and control it with the same foot they pass with. Players follow their pass to take up position at the next cone.

Coaching Points
1. Create space by checking before receiving the pass.
2. At this angle the players should have the correct body to shape to allow the ball to run across their body to receive and pass with the back foot.

Progression
1. You can use 2 balls depending on the number and ability of the players.

Passing Diamond (3) with Quick Combination Play   20 min

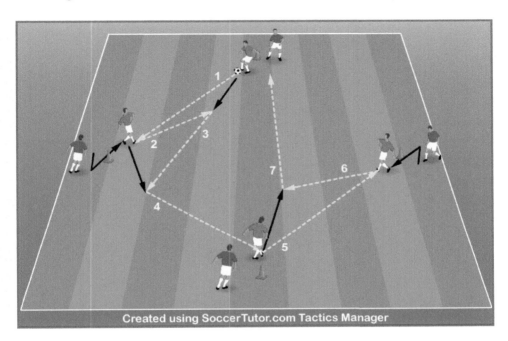

Created using SoccerTutor.com Tactics Manager

Objective
To develop passing, receiving and quick combination play.

Description
In a field area of 15 x 15 yards players are in groups of 8 forming a diamond shape.

We work on the 2 typical passing options, first the one-two after playing the ball to the opposite player and secondly a deep pass looking for the third player after support from the fourth teammate.

Practice in both directions so that both feet are worked. All players receive the ball on the move and control it with the same foot they pass with. Players move to next cone after their last pass.

Coaching Points
1. The timing of the pass is key, making sure the ball is played ahead of the next player to run onto.
2. Use a half-turn body shape and the back foot to pass and receive.

Passing Rectangle (1): Short and Long Support Play   20 min

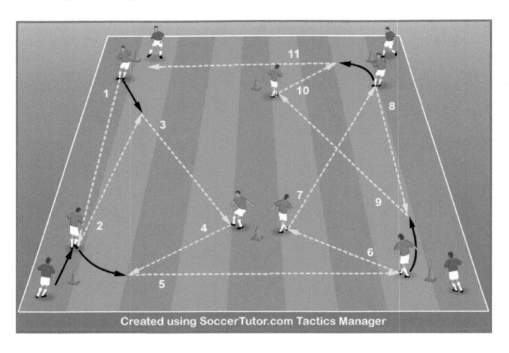

Created using SoccerTutor.com Tactics Manager

Objective

To improve passing, receiving and movements needed to provide support.

Description

In a field area of 30 x 20 yards players are in groups of 11 in a rectangle shape.

Start with 2 balls in opposite corners. The drill is about keeping the ball moving through both short and long passes, incorporating **"support play."** Rotate positions often.

Coaching Points

1. The timing of the pass and support is key, making sure the ball is played ahead of the next player to run onto and the supporting movement is timed well, not too early!

2. Encourage the players to receive the ball half turned with their head up to best see the next pass.

3. Make sure the players communicate with their teammates and keep eye contact.

Passing Rectangle (2): Short and Long Support

20 min

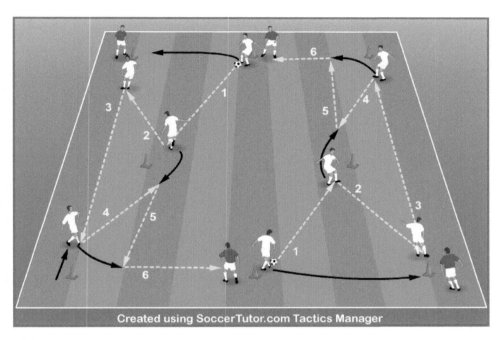

Created using SoccerTutor.com Tactics Manager

Objective

To improve passing, receiving and movements needed to provide support.

Description

In a field area of 30 x 20 yards players are in groups of 12 in a rectangle shape.

Start with 2 balls in opposite corners. The drill is about keeping the ball moving through both short and long passes, incorporating "support". Rotate positions often.

Coaching Points

1. The players and the ball should be constantly moving.

2. Encourage the players to receive the ball half turned with their head up to best see the next pass.

3. Speed up play: Limit the players to 1 touch.

4. Make sure the players communicate with their teammates and keep eye contact.

Passing 'T' with Quick Combination Play

20 min

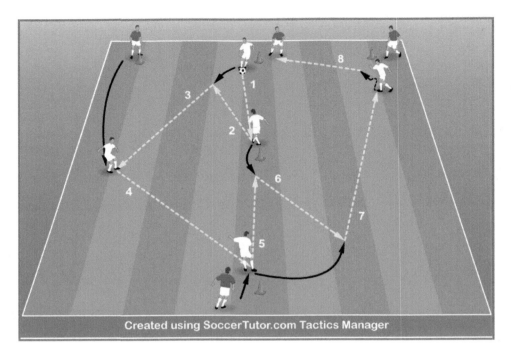

Created using SoccerTutor.com Tactics Manager

Objective
To improve passing, receiving and movements needed to combine quickly.

Description
Use a field area of 20 x 15 yards.

Start with a ball in the centre playing short diagonal passes to the outside areas in the sequence shown in the diagram. Rotate positions often.

Coaching Points
1. Players should work hard to support the player facing them who is passing the ball.
2. Players should check away to create space before moving to meet the pass.
3. Encourage the players to receive the ball half turned with their head up to best see the next pass.

Short Quick Passing Combination

15 min

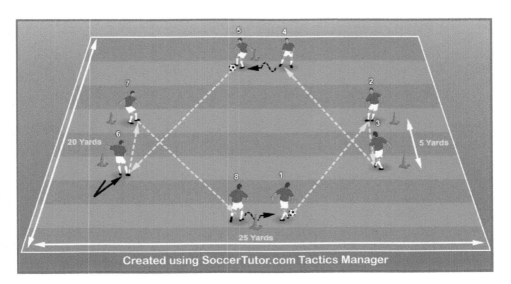

Created using SoccerTutor.com Tactics Manager

Objective

To improve passing, receiving and movements needed to provide support.

Description

Use a field area of 25 x 20 yards and play for 8 minutes in each direction

This practice uses 2 balls and we play diagonal and short passing combinations as shown in the diagram. The player moves quickly to where they have played the ball, ensuring a good dynamic support.

Coaching Points

1. Players should use the inside of the foot for the short passes as it is the most controlled and accurate way.

2. This exercise needs to be performed at a high pace as there are 2 balls.

3. For this passing sequence to be quick, players should check away before moving to receive the pass, which creates space making it easier for the players to play with 1 touch.

Short and Long One-Touch Combination Play (1)   16 min

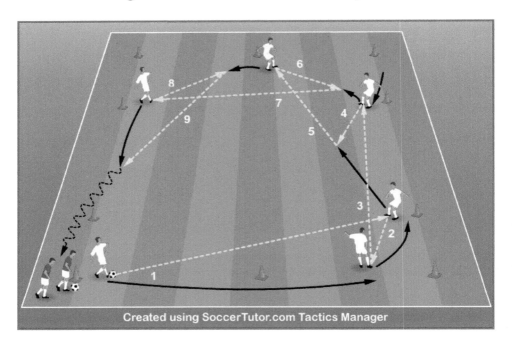

Created using SoccerTutor.com Tactics Manager

Objective
To improve short and long passing, combination play and timing of movements needed to provide support.

Description
Use a field area of 60 x 45 yards and play for 8 minutes in each direction

These long and short passes should utilise both feet and different parts of the foot to be successful in the various situations.

Coaching Points
1. For this passing sequence to be quick and flow effeciently, players should check away before moving to receive the pass, which creates space making it easier for the players to play with 1 touch
2. Use the part of the foot suitable for the distances in each part of the drill and the players must anticipate the next movement to make it flow.
3. The players and the ball should be constantly moving.

Short and Long One-Touch Combination Play (2)   16 min

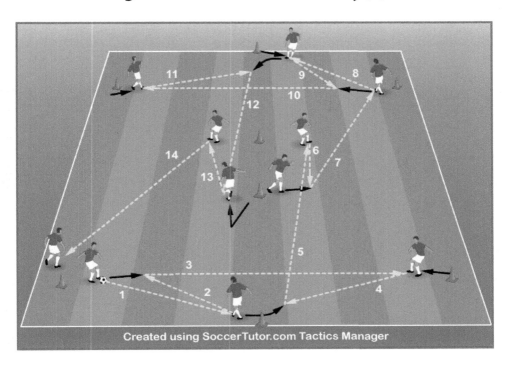

Created using SoccerTutor.com Tactics Manager

Objective

To improve short and long passing, combination play and timing of movements needed to provide support.

Description

Use a field area of 40 x 30 yards and play for 8 minutes in each direction

Short and medium range passes are used. The player runs to where they will play their second pass having played as support. It is important that the players anticipate well so that they can subsequently play an accurate and tight pass.

Coaching Points

1. For this passing sequence to be quick and flow efficiently, players should check away before moving to receive the pass, this creates space making it easier for the players to play one-touch
2. Use the part of the foot suitable for the distances in each part of the drill and the players must anticipate the next movement to make it flow.
3. The players and the ball should be constantly moving.

One-Touch Passing and Combination Play

10 min

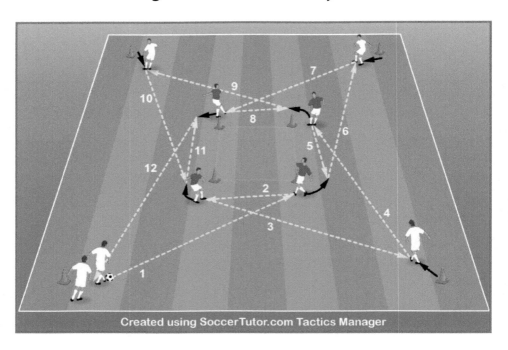

Created using SoccerTutor.com Tactics Manager

Objective
To improve one-touch passing, combination play and timing of movements needed to provide support.

Description
Use a field area of 25 x 20 yards. Within the space perform a drill to practice 1 touch passing using the inside of the foot.

The players must move in the direction they played the pass so there is a good dynamic support and relationship. Work both sides to improve and help the players dominate passes with both feet.

Coaching Points
1. For this passing sequence to be quick and flow efficiently, players should check away before moving to receive the pass, this creates space making it easier for the players to play one-touch

2. Use the part of the foot suitable for the distances in each part of the drill and the players must anticipate the next movement to make it flow.

Possession with Attack/Defence Transition Play

2-15 min

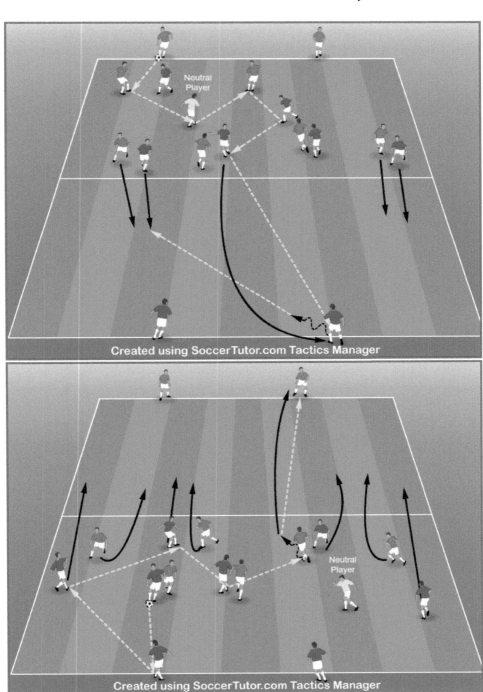

Objective

To develop team possession and quick transition play (attack/defence).

Description

In a 40 x 35 yard area divided into 2 we play possession football in one half with a situation of 8 v 6 (+1 utility player) using a maximum of 2 touches.

If the defending team recovers the ball in this half they aim to move it quickly to the 2 utility players in the opposite area and therefore all of the players move to the other square minus the 2 opposing side players. We call this an attack/defence transition.

The player that makes the pass to the side player on their team swaps places with them.

Coaching Points

1. Encourage players to receive passes half-turned. This enables them to develop their awareness which allows for quicker and better decision making.

2. The defending team needs to press collectively to win the ball back (one closing down the ball with the others marking or preventing the possible passes being made).

Possession, Transition Play and Interchange   20 min

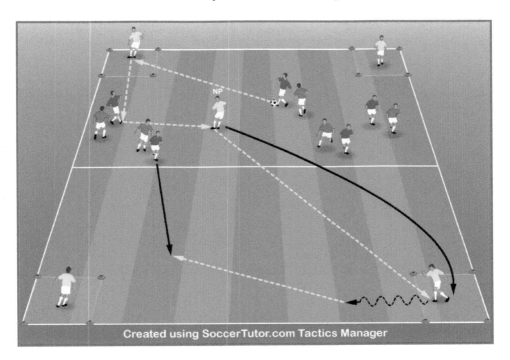

Created using SoccerTutor.com Tactics Manager

Objective
To develop team possession and quick transition play with interchange of positions.

Description
In a 40 x 40 yard space, divide into two 20 x 40 yard rectangles. Play a game of possession in one of the rectangles (5 v 5). The 5 utility players play with the team in possession. This is determined by who plays the ball to them.

If the team in possession manages to play the ball to o ne of the squares in the opposite rectangle all of the players move to play in that area. You can only use the utility players a maximum of twice within one rectangle The player who makes a successful pass to a utility player in the other rectangle must swap places with them.

Coaching Points
1. When the corner players receive the ball they need their teammates to make supporting angled runs to the the left and right of them.

2. Quick combinations should be used with passes made into the path of oncoming teammates.

Possession and Transition Game with Goalkeepers   15 min

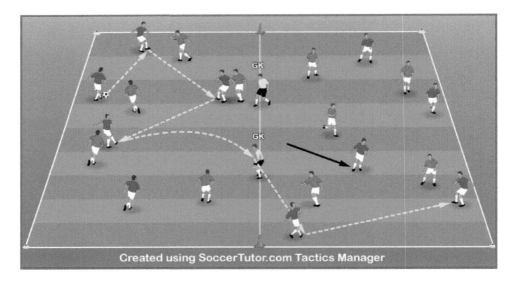

Objective
To develop passing, possession and quick transition play .

Description
Keep possession in a 40 x 30 metre space using a maximum of 2 touches and play 10 v 10. Divide the playing area in half with the 2 goalkeepers on the halfway line dividing the areas. In each area there it is 5 v 5.

After 3 passes they can pass to the keeper who plays it to the other group who must move to receive the ball. If they manage this transition they receive a point.

Coaching Points
1. Movement of players and passing must be done as quickly as possible.
2. Correct body shape (open up on the half-turn) and positioning is important to view the options for where the next pass is going.
3. The defending team needs to press collectively to win the ball back (one closing down the ball with the others marking or preventing the possible passes being made).

Possession and Wide Play Small Sided Game

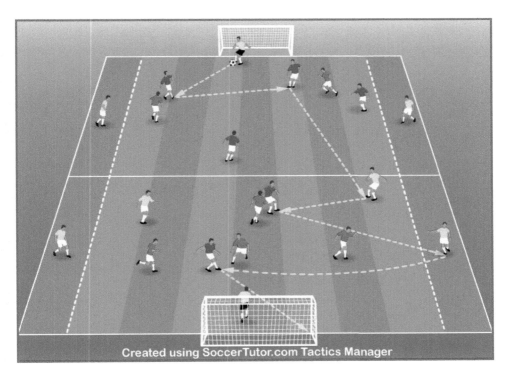

Created using SoccerTutor.com Tactics Manager

Objective
To develop possession, in central and wide areas with crossing and finishing.

Description
Using half pitch divided into 2 sections, 3 teams of 6 play. The aim is to move forward quickly to score a goal. Use a maximum of 2 touches in their own half and use free play in the opposition half.

The third team plays 4 outside and 2 inside as utility players. The team in possession must use at least 1 of the inside utility players (who only play in the attacking half) and at least 1 side player (who must remain in their sections) before shooting.

Coaching Points
1. Players inside should look to quickly switch play the ball to the wide players.
2. In the attacking half players should time the runs well and attack the ball on the move.

Possession Game with Transition and Support Play   15 min

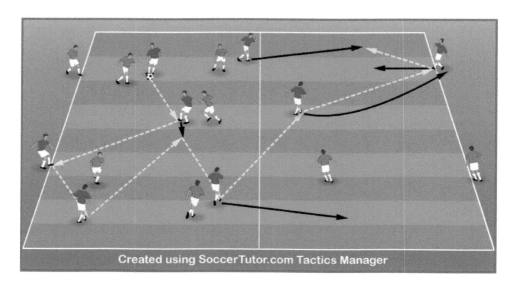

Created using SoccerTutor.com Tactics Manager

Objective
To develop ball possession, passing, transitional play and support.

Description
Using an area of 50 x 30 metres we have 2 zones. We play 8 v 8 with 2 side players each and 1 more player each in the non-active half waiting.

After 5 passes (maximum of 6) the team in possession aims to pass to this non-active player in space in the other zone. The player that plays the pass to the side player takes their place. All the players move across to this zone except for the side players and 1 more player on each team.

The team again aims to make 5 passes before moving again. If the ball is stolen that team remains on that one side of the pitch to reach 5 passes before changing zones.

Coaching Points
1. Make sure the players communicate with their teammates and heads are up.
2. Passes must be quick and accurate due to the limited space.
3. Correct body shape (open up on the half-turn) and positioning is important to view where the next pass can be played.
4. The defending team needs to press collectively to win the ball back (one closing down the ball with the others marking or preventing the possible passes being made).
5. When the ball is intercepted teammates need to be very quick to offer immediate support to the left and right of the player in possession.

Build-Up Play from the Back in 8 v 8 SSG

24 min

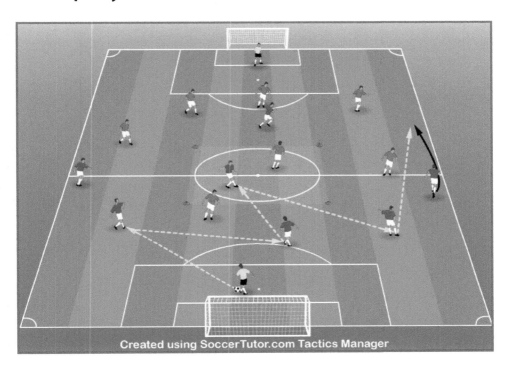

Created using SoccerTutor.com Tactics Manager

Objective
To develop combination play starting from deep in defence.

Description
In two 12 minutes halves we play on a full pitch with a defined square as shown on the diagram.

It is mostly free play although they must play through the centres in order to progress and attack into the opposition's half. For older players, use central midfield players in the square.

Coaching Points
1. The players should play quickly with 1 or 2 touches.
2. Create space and strive to get away from your marker.
3. Movement into space will also create space for teammates to exploit as well as providing you with an opportunity to receive the ball.

2 v 1/3 v 2: Defence to Attack Transition

14 min

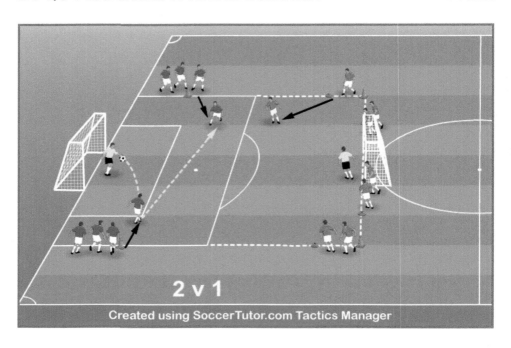

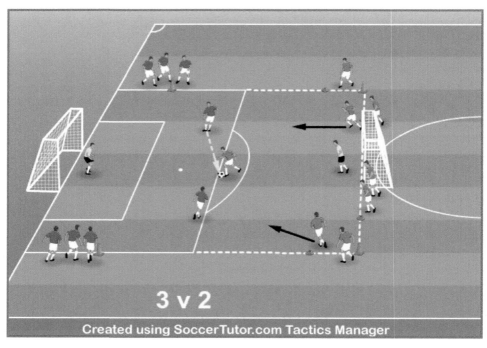

Objective

To develop and practice attacking combinations using the numerical advantage of 2 v 1 or 3 v 2, as well as the defenders positioning themselves correctly.

Description

In a space double the size of the penalty area, 2 teams of 8 players play a finishing game.

This finishing drill starts with a 2 v 1 situation originating from the keeper. If the 1 defender manages to steal the ball, then 2 teammates quickly join to make a quick transition of 3 v 2 in the opposite direction.

Coaching Points

1. The attackers should use quick one-two combinations to get in behind the defender.
2. If there is a clear opportunity to shoot, take it quickly.
3. Movement into space will also create space for teammates to exploit as well as providing you with an opportunity to receive the ball.

Numerical Advantage 12 v 6 Small Sided Game

20 min

Objective
To develop and exploit a numerical advantage to create fast attacks.

Description
In a space double the size of the penalty area 2 teams of 6 play with 6 more utility players outside the space. Inside the area play 2 touch football and outside is always 1 touch.

If a goal is scored or 5 minutes elapses change the teams around. The winning team remains and the others swap with the utility players and take up their positions outside the area.

Coaching Points
1. Play and think quickly.
2. Players should be constantly moving into space to receive the ball and utilising the side players to fully exploit the numerical advantage.
3. If there Is an opportunity to shoot, take it.

9 v 9 Three Zone Small Sided Game

2-12 mins per game

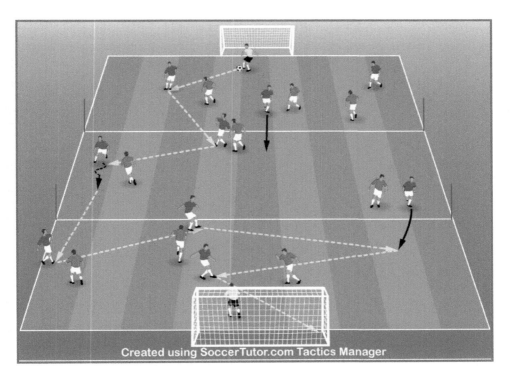

Created using SoccerTutor.com Tactics Manager

Objective
To develop specific roles and positions in team play.

Description
Using an area of 50 x 45 metres we play 9 v 9 in 3 limited zones that the players must respect. The team that attacks can move 1 player from the previous zone into the next zone to achieve a numerical superiority.

Coaching Points
1. Passing and movement needs to be as quick as possible.
2. The passes need to be out in front of the oncoming player who must be moving forwards to keep the ball moving at all times.
3. Encourage: Running into space, third man runs, overlaps and communication.
4. The defending team needs to press collectively, maintaining the correct positions in their different zones.

2 v 1/1 v 2 Attacking and Defending Duels

20 min

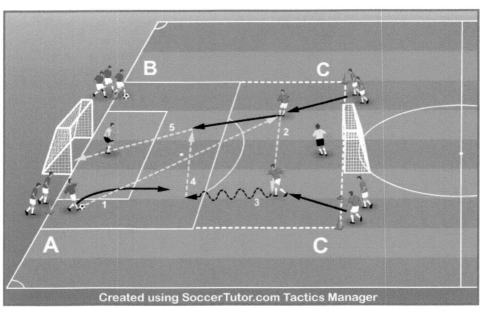

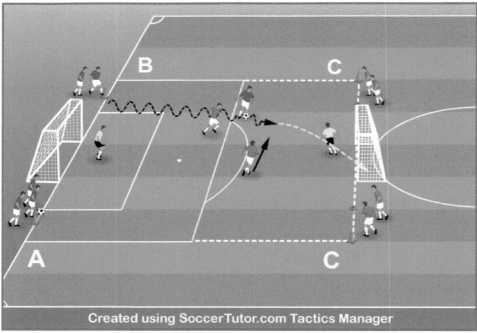

Objective

To develop and practice attacking scenarios with an advantage or disadvantage.

Description

Outside an area twice the size of the penalty area, line the players up 3 per line in the positions shown in the diagram. The players in A play the ball to a player in area C who faces up to the player in A in a 2 v 1 with another teammate from C on the opposite side.

When the two C players reach player A, a player from B dribbles from the side towards the other goal and the players in C become defenders and a 1 v 2 situation develops. Swap the positions after 10 minutes.

Coaching Points

1. Both C players should use quick one-two combinations to get in behind the defender.
2. Player B needs to act very quickly using feints/moves to beat the defenders and get a shot on goal.
3. If there is a clear opportunity to shoot, all players need to take it.
4. When defending in the 1 v 2 one must go toward the player, while the other defender covers the space in behind

Fast Break Attack vs Defence Practices

20 min

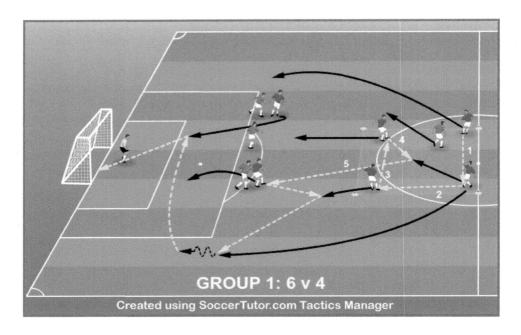

GROUP 1: 6 v 4

Created using SoccerTutor.com Tactics Manager

Objective
To develop fast break attacking from deep in midfield.

Description
This attack vs defence drill is in 2 groups with each group using half the pitch. The players use a maximum of 2 touches in all parts of the exercise.

Group 1
Players must make 4 successful passes within the square before being able to enter the half pitch. There is then a scenario of 6 attackers v 4 defenders.

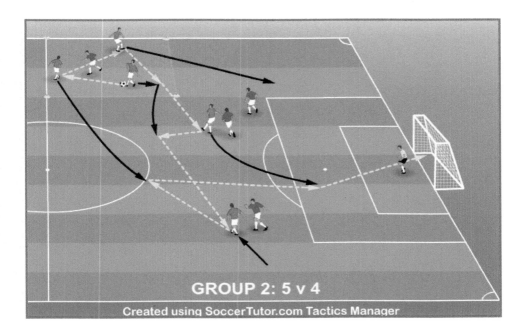

GROUP 2: 5 v 4

Created using SoccerTutor.com Tactics Manager

Group 2

Players in the square must make 3 successful passes before being able to enter the half pitch. There is then a scenario with 5 attackers v 4 defenders.

Coaching Points

1. With the numerical advantage, the attackers should make forward movements to stretch the defence and create gaps to exploit.
2. Players need get away from their markers to receive the ball.
3. Players can really utilise the full width along with the numerical advantage.

9 v 9 Six Zone Small Sided Game

14 min

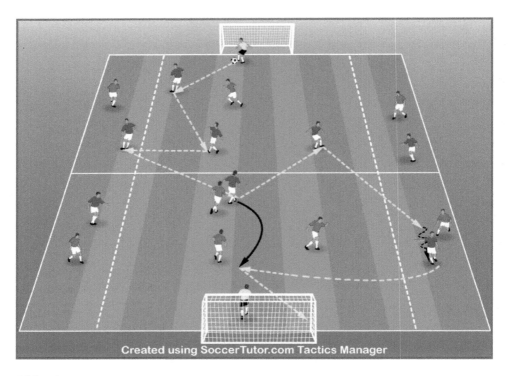

Created using SoccerTutor.com Tactics Manager

Objective
To develop specific roles and positions in team play.

Description
We play two halves of 7 minutes. Play a 9 v 9 match from box to box with 6 zones marked out and the players can only play in the area ahead of them.

Coaching Points
1. Passing and movement needs to be as quick as possible.
2. The players should receive half-turned for the transition to flow more easily.
3. Utilising the side players is key to advancing up the pitch, making the most of the numerical advantage.

5 v 5 + 2 + 4 Dynamic Possession Game

18 min

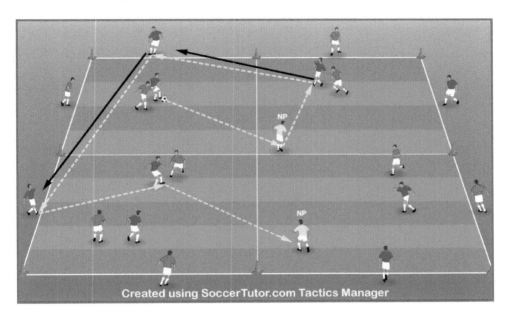

Created using SoccerTutor.com Tactics Manager

Objective

To practice retaining possession - passing, receiving and creating space.

Description

In an area 45 x 40 metres we play an 5 v 5 + 2 neutral players possession game with each team having 4 supporting players outside as shown in the diagram. The 2 neutral players within the square play with the team in possession.

Each time a player makes a pass to a teammate on the outside they should swap positions with them. Play 2 touch football so that it is more dynamic.

Coaching Points

1. Make sure players keep their heads up to be aware of teammates' positions.
2. When creating space, players should check away with an open body shape before moving to receive the pass.
3. The body should open up when receiving, with the first touch and pass made with the back foot.

9 v 9 Counter Attacking Small Sided Game

24 min

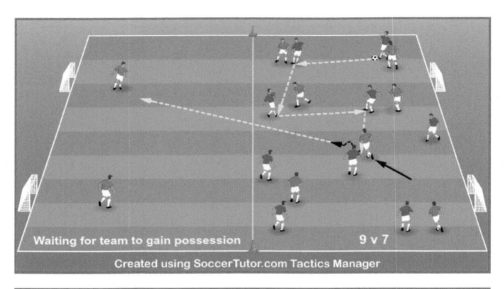

Waiting for team to gain possession

9 v 7

Created using SoccerTutor.com Tactics Manager

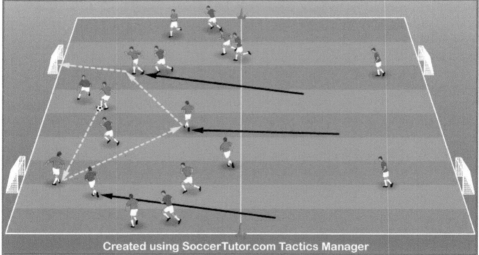

Created using SoccerTutor.com Tactics Manager

Objective

To develop counter attacks, supporting the forwards high up the pitch.

Description

In an area of 50 x 40 metres the field is split into 2 sections, as we play 12 minutes per half.

We play 9 v 9. The game starts in the middle of one of the areas where you should play 9 v 7. In the other area of the pitch 2 teammates of the defending team wait for their team to steal the ball and pass to them (quickly developing a counter-attack).

When these players receive the ball in the other section, they should wait until their teammates join them and play the ball backwards first before developing an attack of their own. The team move 7 of their players across to defend, leaving 2 to wait.

Coaching Points

1. Encourage players to receive passes half-turned. This enables them to develop their awareness which allows for quicker and better decision making.

2. The defending team needs to press collectively to win the ball back (one closing down the ball with the others marking or preventing the possible passes being made).

3 Team Possession and Transition Game

15 min

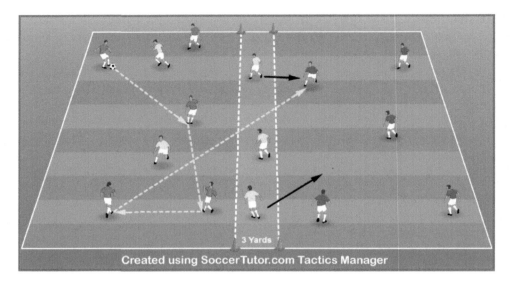

3 Yards

Created using SoccerTutor.com Tactics Manager

Objective

To develop ball possession, speed of play and transitioning.

Description

3 teams play in a 40 x 30 metre area. In one of the lateral zones play 5 v 2. The team in possession must pass the ball a minimum of 3 times before transferring it to a different zone.

The 2 players try to regain possession and if they do not manage this before the ball is passed to the other zone they both move to the central zone as 2 of the players from the central zone move to apply pressure. A new 5 v 2 scenario is created in the other zone.

The players in the central zone are there to try and intercept passes between the other 2 zones.

Coaching Points

1. Make sure when the teams need to change roles it is done quickly to maintain cohesion and keep the exercise flowing smoothly.

2. The 2 defending players need to be clever and work together well, with 1 closing down the ball carrier and the other trying to intercept the pass.

3. The team in possession need to constantly move to get away from markers and should be able to create space and utilise numerical advantage.

Dynamic 4 Zone Possession Game

15 min

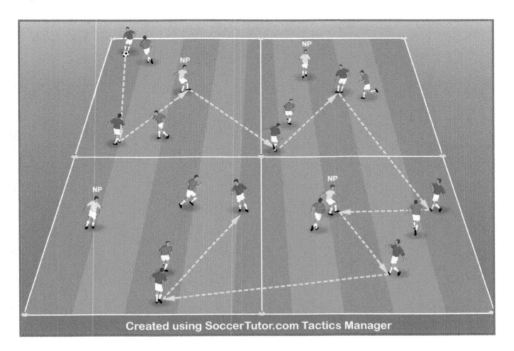

Created using SoccerTutor.com Tactics Manager

Objective
To develop ball possession - receiving, short, medium and long passing.

Description
In a big 50 x 50 metre square divided into four 25 x 25 metre squares we have a drill with 2 teams of 8 players divided into pairs occupying each square The team in possession is supported by 4 neutral players. They must also remain in the 1 square.

To make the drill more dynamic players are not able to play back to the same square they received the ball from.

Coaching Points
1. All players need to keep moving, especially when attempting to receive the ball from a different zone.
2. With 3 v 2 situations players should strive to form a triangle, with the 2 supporting players moving either side of the ball carrier.

Playing Wide and Switching Play in a SSG

24 min

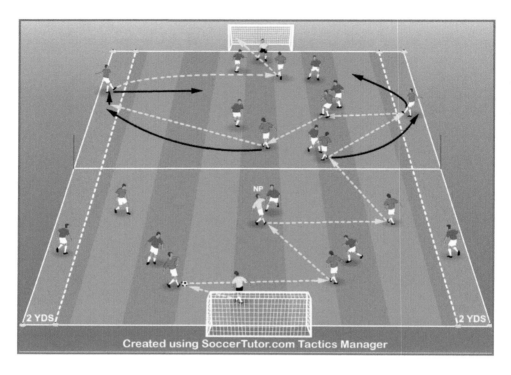

Created using SoccerTutor.com Tactics Manager

Objective

To develop playing out wide and tactical switching of play - quick interchanges, crossing and finishing.

Description

We play two 12 minute halves in a 40 x 40 metre area playing 10 v 10 with 1 extra neutral player.

The aim is to get the ball wide in the opposition half and finish the move by switching play to the opposite side. When the wide players receive a pass from a teammate they exchange positions with them. The emphasis of the drill is to play inside to draw the opponents in and then play wide.

Coaching Points

1. The speed of play needs to be high to switch play effectively.
2. The use of 1 touch when possible can be key in successful switches of play.
3. The runs from deep need to be well timed to meet the final cross and attack it.
4. When switching, centre players need to create space in front and behind the ball.

9 v 4 Zonal Possession and Support Play Game

36 min

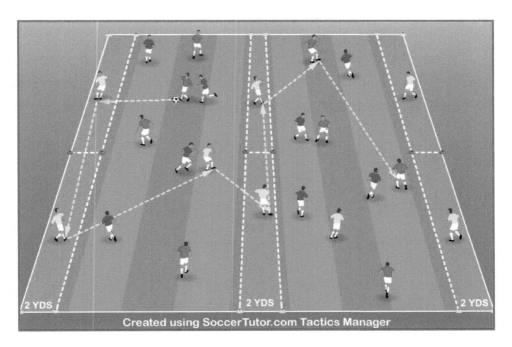

2 YDS   2 YDS   2 YDS

Created using SoccerTutor.com Tactics Manager

Objective
To develop ball possession - receiving, short, medium and long passing.

Description
In an area of 50 x 45 metres, 3 teams of 8 players are divided into 3 different zones.

The 2 teams playing in the main sections have 4 players in each section with the aim of keeping possession.

Those in the 2 metre wide channels are utility players and support the team in possession, as well as 2 more utility player in each of the 2 main sections. All the utility players should be mobile and be level with the play. The utility players in the channels should support each other and make short passes between themselves.

Coaching Points
1. The players should be constantly moving, making supporting movements.
2. They should move in semi-circles to escape markers and create space to receive.
3. The defending team needs to communicate well to press cohesively.

CHAPTER 4

IVÁN MADROÑO CAMPOS

Real Madrid Academy Coach

REAL MADRID ACADEMY COACH PROFILE

Iván Madroño Campos
Real Madrid Academy Coach

- National Football Coach (Level III)
- Bachelor's degree in Physical Education and Sports
- Teaching degree in Physical Education
- Master of Physical Preparation in Football (APF-RFEF)

Exercises to improve technique in the Youth team stage.

As a starting point for the justification for the development of practical work, we will begin by mentioning some technical definitions from various authors, both for individual and team sports.

This allows us to appreciate the differences between the conception of technique analysed from the perspective of individual sports and the conception of technique analysed from a team sports standpoint.

"Basic procedure of the motor speciality of a modality or discipline, separate from the person and operationalised, whose function is to serve as an ideal target for action and training". *(Martin, 1979, quoted by Neumaier and cols, 2002).*

"Technique as an ideal model of a sports movement based on knowledge and practical experience". *(Grosser and Neumaier 1986, Weineck, 1988).*

"Technique is the specific way of performing a physical exercise, with the motor structure being the predominant characteristic that differentiates the different activities". *(Bompa, 1990).*

"We understand sporting technique to be the determining factor in athletic performance that includes all rational movements leading to an athlete that is functional, economical and adapted to obtaining excellent results in sports competition under the current rules". *(Morante, 1994 c, Morante and Izquierdo 2008).*

"They are all those actions that a football player can perform dominating and directing the ball with all contact surfaces permitted by the regulations. If the result benefits a single player it is known as individual technique and if it benefits everybody it is known as team technique". *(Spanish Football Federation Coaching School).*

Given these definitions from various authors it is clear that in every sport the importance of technique carries a weight that is different to that of the performance. Focusing on football, we find that the importance of the technique is more relevant to good decision making.

Continuing the argument, you could say that technical movements in football are not subject to rigid and closed motor patterns but to correct decision making and the success of the technical action or actions that allow the player to make a decision, even wrong ones, are in relation to ideal and successful motor patterns in terms of result and performance.

As a fundamental idea of everything developed to this point, in football we speak of technique at the service of the tactics, so they should never be developed as separate components but should be complementary to each other. In this sense, we must reflect this fundamental idea in the technical training.

In respect to the category that we are concerned with, the Youth team, we have to take into account that the players have already been through various stages of training and should be free thinking and have assimilated motor control in different contexts that allows them to identify and resolve changing situations in an ever changing sport such as ours.

In the early stages of football, the technical training is more analytical, through which, using repetition and methodological progression, the training goes from simple to complex allowing the player to assimilate those patterns or motor skills which later allow them to resolve complex situations within the game.

Here, as we approach the Youth category, the analytical technical training declines as a percentage in favour of more comprehensive training and more complex drills and, as a result of this evolution, the number of stimuli is increased and the decision making becomes more difficult and there is greater cognitive demand. In summary, training is more complex and repetition and mechanization of actions becomes more prominent.

Finally, after the theoretical justification of technical work with the Youth team, we are going to briefly explain how we classify the different drills that have been developed. We will distinguish two main groups within which all methods of training fall: game play and non game play.

Non game play: passing exercises, combined actions, shooting exercises and ability games without opposition.

Game play: possession with/without orientation, possession with finishing, restricted games, modified games etc

Technical Dribbling Exercises 12 min

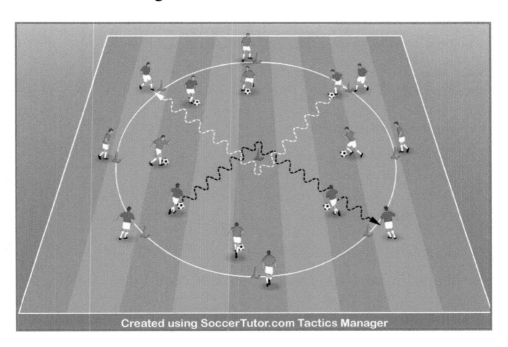

Objective
To improve dribbling with both feet and peripheral vision.

Description
Use a circle 40 metres in diameter. Play three 4 minutes drills.

1. Free option without obstacles

- Dribbling backwards and forwards
- Dribbling to another cone (not the one facing them)
- Dribbling and going around a cone with the foot that best suits the turn
- Dribbling with the weaker foot

2. Competition option (Increase the speed)

- Relays to and from the cone situated in front competing against other teams
- Relays back and forward with the weak foot
- Relays in pairs (competition between teams)
- Relays in pairs with 2 balls

3. Option with opposition

- Dribble into the middle circle and turn back avoiding the defenders
- Dribble to a cone in the other half of the field after crossing a circle full of defenders

Coaching Points
1. The players need to dribble with their head up, never looking at the ball.
2. The players need to be aware of the other players dribbling to the middle cone, making sure to avoid them.
3. Make sure the players use all different parts of the feet to dribble - laces, inside, outside, sole.
4. The ball should be kept as close to the feet as possible at all times during the exercise.

1 v 1 - Beating the Defender   10 min

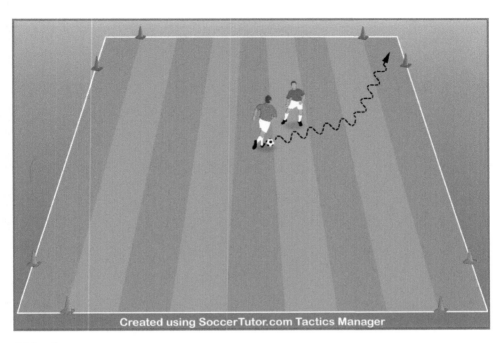

Created using SoccerTutor.com Tactics Manager

Objective
To improve dribbling, faints/moves, pressing forward and playing down the flank.

Description
In a 15 x 10 metre area with 1 metre wide goals we play five 2 minute rounds.

In a limited space each player attacks and defends 2 mini goals. A goal is scored by dribbling the ball through the cones.

Coaching Points
1. Keep the ball moving in the opposite direction to where the defender attempts to challenge.
2. The attacker needs to demonstrate explosive acceleration.

1 v 1 : Beating the Defender (2)   10 min

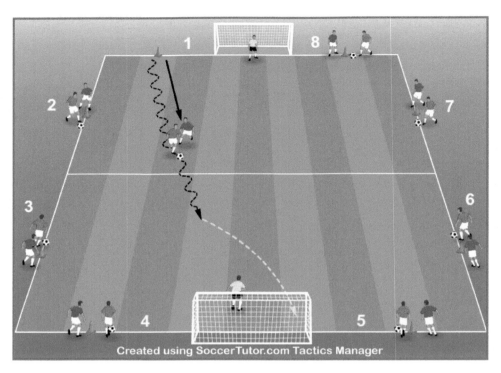

Created using SoccerTutor.com Tactics Manager

Objective

To improve dribbling, faints/moves, pressing forward and shooting/finishing.

Description

In a space double the penalty area each player has time for 2 turns each.

2 teams face up with players in pairs as shown in the diagram. In an established order, the player in the first pair attacks the goal. The defender tries to react quickly without setting off before the player with the ball.

The players on the goal line must attack the opposite goal while the players down the lines can attack either goal. The next pair sets off after the previous pair has finished their movement.

Coaching Points

1. The attacker player needs to utilise the space in behind the defender.
2. The attacker needs to demonstrate explosive acceleration.

Aerial Control and Passing

10-15 min

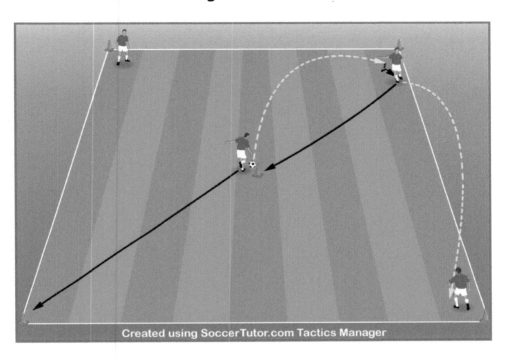

Created using SoccerTutor.com Tactics Manager

Objective

To improve control and striking the ball with the correct volleying technique.

Description

In an area of 10 x 10 metres we have 4 players inside a square with 5 markers (one of which is free). The player in the middle starts with the ball and plays a high ball to the teammate of his choice and runs to the free marker. The next player plays a high ball to a teammate and moves to the free marker which is in the centre. The same sequence continues.

Each player starts with 10 points. Every time the ball touches the ground the player that let it fall loses a point. The player with the highest points total at the end wins. You can play with free touches or a maximum of 2 -3 depending on the ability level.

Coaching Points

1. The players should try to use all parts of the foot, thigh, chest and head to maximize control of the ball.

2. Start with a slow pace of aerial pass until consistency of quality is produced. Then the tempo can be increased.

Passing 'Star' - Pass, Receive and Move

12 min

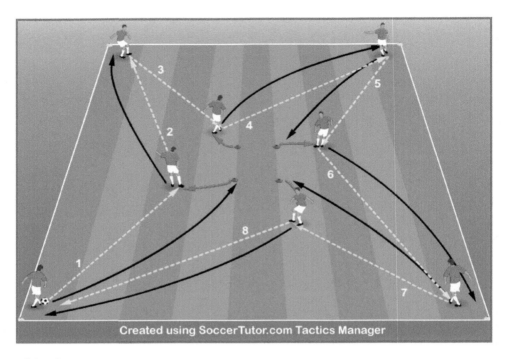

Created using SoccerTutor.com Tactics Manager

Objective

To develop passing with both feet and receiving with 1 foot and pass with the other.

Description

In a 40 x 40 metre square we play two 6 minute periods.

The players are positioned as shown in the diagram and play the passes in the order provided on the diagram. In rotation the players go to the position where they passed the ball. Players check off the cones when receiving replicating a movement away from a defender to create space.

Coaching Points

1. When receiving with 1 foot and passing with the other, the first touch needs to be well judged to go across the body to receive the pass with first touch towards the direction to pass the ball.

2. Improve the speed of play by limiting the players to 1 touch when possible.

Passing 'Y' Shape - Quick Combination + Dribble   12 min

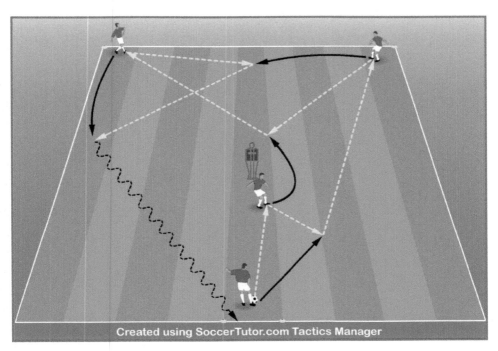

Created using SoccerTutor.com Tactics Manager

Objective
To develop passing and receiving with both feet during combination play.

Description
With 20 metres between players we play 2 periods of 6 minutes.

The players line up in a Y shape and play the passes as shown in the diagram. The player moves to the next position after playing the pass.

Coaching Points
1. When receiving with 1 foot and passing with the other the first touch needs to be well judged and pushed out in front of the body.
2. Reduce the time between the first touch and the pass, and then progress to 1 touch when possible.
3. Passes in the combinations need to be weighted well and aimed in front of the teammate so they can run onto the ball.
4. The passing and dribbling should be done at a high tempo.

1 and 2 Touch Passing Combinations

12 min

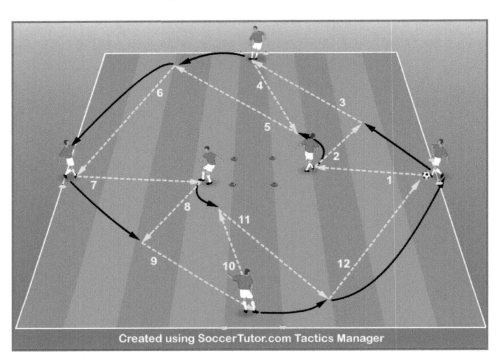

Created using SoccerTutor.com Tactics Manager

Objective
To develop passing combinations at various angles.

Description
With 20 metres between players we play 2 periods of 6 minutes.

The players take up their positions and play the passes as shown in the diagram. 2 balls are played at the same time from opposite sides of the playing area (Start from position 1 and 7). The player moves to the next position after playing their last pass.

Coaching Points
1. The players and the ball should be constantly moving.
2. For this passing sequence to be quick and flow efficiently, players should check away before moving to receive the pass, this creates space making it easier for the players to play one-touch
3. Make sure the players communicate with their teammates and keep eye contact.

Short and Long Passing Combination Play

12 min

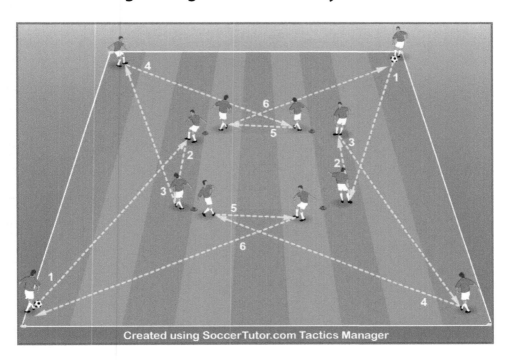

Objective

To develop short and long combination play.

Description

In a 20 x 40 metre square with a 10 x 10 metres square we play 2 periods of 6 minutes.

The players line up and play the passes as shown in the diagram.

Coaching Points

1. Due to the complexity of the drill the middle players need to adopt a stance that allows them to execute the pass whether the ball is played in front or behind them.
2. The weight of the passes is key, making sure the ball is played ahead of the next player to move onto.
3. All passes need to be as accurate as possible to keep the ball moving quickly.

Passing Combination Play with '2 Routes'

12 min

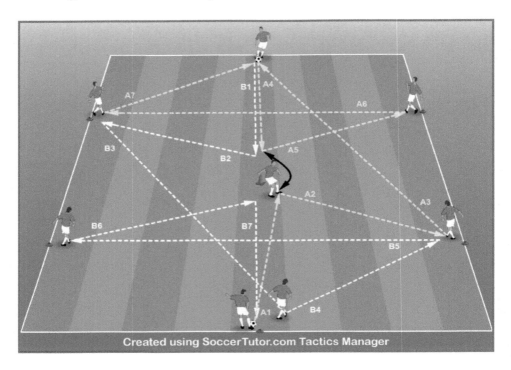

Created using SoccerTutor.com Tactics Manager

Objective
To develop combinations including soft and hard passes.

Description
With 20 metres between players we play 2 periods of 6 minutes.

The players line up as shown in the diagram as 2 balls are used starting from opposite positions. There are 2 different combinations - A & B. The ball is played rapidly to and from the player in the middle who receives the ball from different directions. Everyone except the middle player move to the next position after passing.

Coaching Points
1. Change the player in the middle often.
2. The player in the middle needs to have an open stance to be able to receive passes from all directions.
3. Passes in the combinations need to be weighted well and aimed in front of the teammate so they can run onto the ball.

Player Position Specific Build-up and Combination   12 min

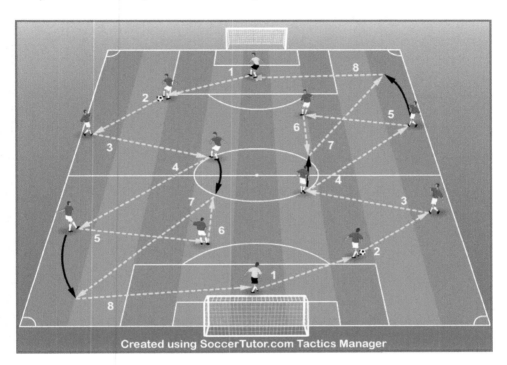

Created using SoccerTutor.com Tactics Manager

Objective
To develop build-up combinations within specified playing positions.

Description
On a full pitch, play two periods of 6 minutes.

The players line up as shown in the diagram playing the passes in the order shown. Play the ball round the whole pitch through the opposite keeper using actions appropriate to the position the player is in.

The players change positions so that they play and make a pass from everywhere during the drill. You can change the distances between the players so they have to change the strength of the passes and the order in which the passes are played.

Coaching Points
1. Body shape should be open on half-turn to see their teammates positions.
2. Player should check to create space before receiving the next pass.
3. The players must play quickly with 1 or 2 touches.

1 v 1 + 2: Beating the Defender and Goalkeeper   10 min

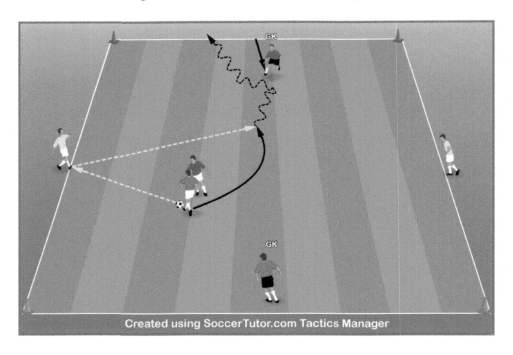

Objective
To improve dribbling, control, feints/moves, pushing forward and playing down the flanks.

Description
In a 15 x 20 metre area we play five 2 minutes periods.

In this limited space we play 1 v 1 plus goalkeepers. The objective is to dribble the ball across the opposite line which is defended by a goalkeeper.

The attacking player has 2 external support players that are offensive utility players and can only play with 1 touch to encourage quick movement.

Coaching Points
1. Encourage quick movement - play a quick one-two combination with one of the utility side players.
2. The attacker should run in behind the defender utilising the space.
3. Be decisive: Beat the defender and goalkeeper positively.

Deep Attacking Combination and Finishing (1)   16 min

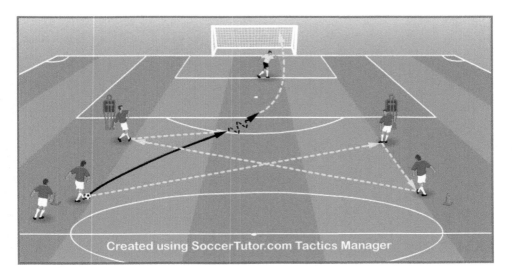

Created using SoccerTutor.com Tactics Manager

Objective
To practice attacking combinations starting from deep in midfield and finishing.

Description
Using half a pitch, play 2 periods of 8 minutes.

Line the players up as shown in the diagram and play the passes shown ending with the starting player shooting on goal. Change the roles of the players often.

Coaching Points
1. Players must play quickly, using just 1 touch when possible.
2. The weight of the final pass and timing of the run needs to be coordinated to make sure the ball is received on the move.
3. Before the shot, the ball may need to be knocked out in front, making sure the player uses short steps straight behind the ball, striking through the middle of it.
4. Get the players to practice different shooting techniques - laces, inside, outside.

Deep Attacking Combination and Finishing (2)   16 min

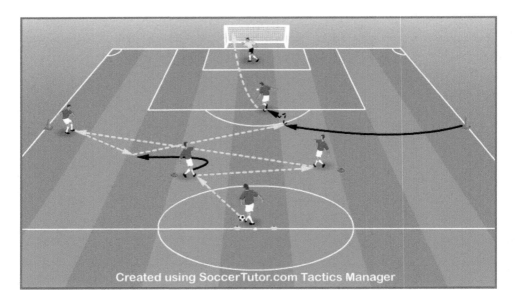

Created using SoccerTutor.com Tactics Manager

Objective

To practice attacking combinations starting from deep in midfield and finishing.

Description

Using half a pitch, we play 2 periods of 8 minutes.

Line the players up as in the diagram and play the passes shown ending with the player timing a run from the cone to shoot on goal.

Coaching Points

1. The final pass needs to weighted well and timed to meet the run so it can be struck first time.
2. The shooting player should practice checking from the cone as to create space/get away from a marker.
3. The practice should use both feet and rotate the roles often.
4. Communication is key in this exercise , with awareness of runs and passes.

Central Finishing Competition (1)

16 min

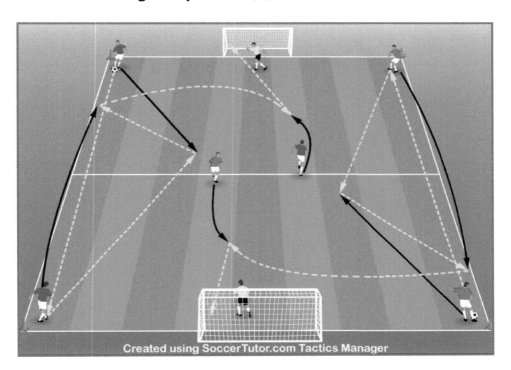

Created using SoccerTutor.com Tactics Manager

Objective
Improves attacking combinations, playing through the centre and various shooting techniques including heading.

Description
In a space double the size of the penalty area we play 2 periods of 8 minutes.

We have a competition between the players in the centre. The players line up as shown in the diagrams in a way that both teams finish facing towards a goal. In the second period change the position of the central player.

A goal scores a point. If a goal is scored from 1 touch it will count as 2 points.

Coaching Points
1. The players need to communicate with the passing combination for when to release the pass on the overlap so it is out in front of them.
2. Attacking players should time the runs well and attack the ball on the run.
3. Vary different parts of the drill to keep players alert and aware:

Cross height - on the floor, waist height and head height

Cross depth - near post, middle and far post

Finishing - shooting technique (laces, inside, outside, volleys and headers).

Central Finishing Competition (2)

16 min

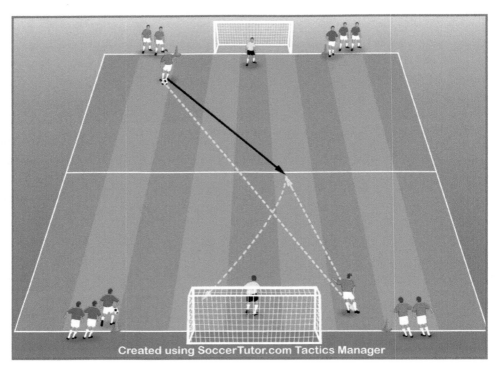

Created using SoccerTutor.com Tactics Manager

Objective
Improves playing through the centre and finishing.

Description
In a space double the size of the penalty area we play 2 periods of 8 minutes.

We again have a competition between the players. They line up as shown in the diagrams with 1 player from 1 side playing a long pass and moving forward to meet the return. In the second period change the position of the pass and the shot. The rotation changes players to the other line of their own team to change roles.

Coaching Points
1. Passes should be of high speed and accurate.
2. Timing of the run must be coordinated to the pass.
3. The shot technique should be varied, depending on the angle in which the player is approaching the ball.
4. Encourage the players to take the shot on with their first touch.

Overlapping Runs, Crossing and Finishing

16 min

Objective

To practice attacking combinations with overlapping wing play, crossing and finishing.

Description

Using half a pitch, we play 2 periods of 8 minutes.

This is a crossing and finishing competition in teams. The players line up as shown in the diagram with the players positioned on 3 markers.

Play the passes as shown and when the outside player crosses the ball the other team start their movement so that they are never stationary. The players change position so they all practice crossing the ball.

Coaching Points

1. The pass out wide should be out in front of the overlapping run.
2. The cross needs to be timed to meet the run.
3. Encourage the players to communicate when running into the box, one going near post and the other far post.

Quick Interplay and Third Man Runs

12 min

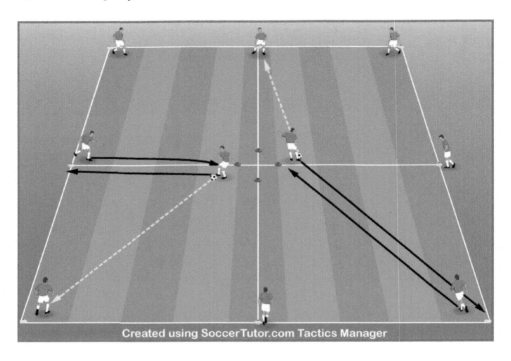

Created using SoccerTutor.com Tactics Manager

Objective
To develop passing, receiving, quick changing of positions and 3rd man runs.

Description
There is 20 metres between players and we play 2 periods of 6 minutes.

The players line up as shown in the diagram and the 2 players on the inside have a ball each. The inside players pass to one of the outer players and change position with a third player who then moves to the middle to receive the return pass.

Coaching Points
1. The player in the middle needs to be half turned when receiving the ball.
2. This player should also control/pass with the back foot.
3. The second pass needs to coordinated with the run of the third player.

'Naught's and Crosses' Game

12 min

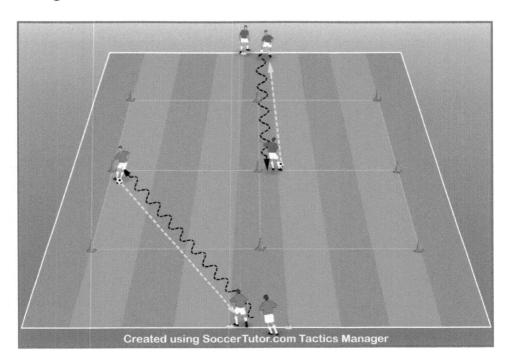

Created using SoccerTutor.com Tactics Manager

Objective
To improve ball control with both feet, accurate passing and quick decision making.

Description
In a 30 x 30 metre square (10 between cones) we play 2 periods of 6 minutes.

Line up the 2 teams of 3 players as shown in the diagram. At a signal, the first player in each team sets off dribbling towards a cone (not the one nearest). Once at a cone they pass back without hitting any of the cones to the next player in their team.

The objective is to get 3 players in a line (vertical, horizontal or diagonal) while reventing your opponents from doing the same.

Coaching Points
1. The pass back has to be fast and accurate as they are competing.
2. The players need to dribble with their head up, never looking at the ball.
3. The players need to be aware of the other players dribbling to cones, making sure to avoid them.
4. The ball should be kept as close to the feet as possible at all times during the exercise. Also, use all different parts of the foot.

'Naught's and Crosses' Game with 1 v 1 Duel   12 min

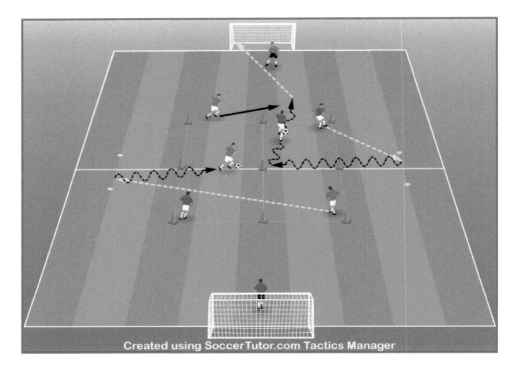

Created using SoccerTutor.com Tactics Manager

Objective

To improve dribbling with both feet, accurate passing, 1 v 1's and shooting.

Description

In the area between both penalty areas, we play 2 periods of 6 minutes.

The same as the previous drill, but this time when one of the teams gets a line the player with the ball on the winning team dribbles quickly to the opposition goal and shoots.

The nearest player on the losing team chases the ball carrier to defend the goal which produces a 1 v 1 duel, with a goalkeeper also.

Coaching Points

1. The players need to dribble with their head up, never looking at the ball.
2. Keep the ball moving in the opposite direction to where the defender attempts to challenge.
3. The attacker needs to demonstrate explosive acceleration.
4. The defender should be side on to the attacker at the appropriate distance, enabling them to respond to the attacker's movement.

Possession, Crossing and Finishing Zonal SSG   18 min

Objective

To improve passing, receiving, crossing and finishing from different areas.

Description

Using a 45 x 40 metres area (3 zones of 15 x 40 metres) we play 3 periods of 6 minutes.

2 teams (4 v 4) play for possession in the middle zone with support from 2 utility players on the outside. When a team manages to bring a utility player into the game they should play a deep ball down the line so that the utility player on that side crosses the ball to be finished by the team that gave them the ball.

The other team must defend the goal using clearances, interceptions and blocks to stop them scoring. Play 2 touches to encourage high speed and dynamic play.

Coaching Points

1. The passes in the middle need to be quick and accurate using 1 touch when possible.
2. The utility player needs to time the cross to the attacker's runs.
3. Body shape needs to be side on facing away from the goal to see the cross coming in to block or clear the ball.

Overlapping Wide Play and Finishing in a SSG

12 min

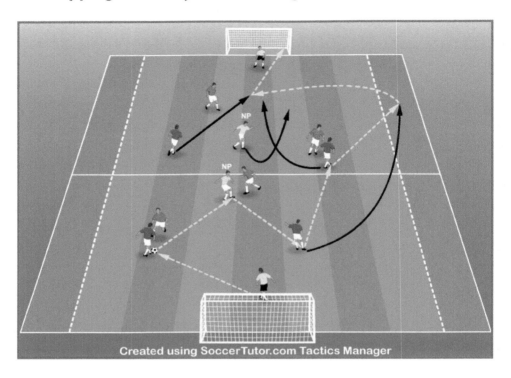

Created using SoccerTutor.com Tactics Manager

Objective
To improve, passing, receiving, overlapping runs, crossing and finishing.

Description
In an area double the size of the penalty area we play 4 periods of 3 minutes.

2 teams of 4 players face each other with 2 utility players joining the team in possession.

2 players from each team and 1 utility player are allowed in each half.

A goalkeeper plays the ball out to a player who tries to connect with a teammate in the other half of the playing area. When this is achieved, the teammate from the first area must run down the wing to play a cross for one of their 3 teammates to finish.

Coaching Points
1. The players need to communicate well for when to release the pass on the overlap so it is weighted perfectly and out in front of the player moving forward.
2. The player crossing needs to time the cross to the attacker's runs.
3. When defending the cross the body shape needs to be side on facing away from the goal to see the cross coming in to block or clear the ball.

Quick Interplay and Dynamic Finishing Drill   16 min

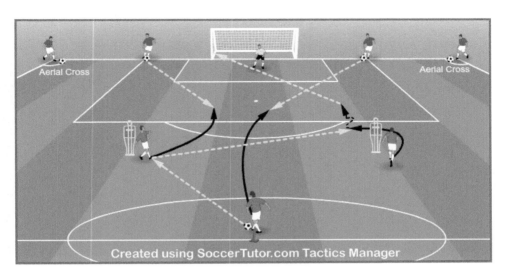

Created using SoccerTutor.com Tactics Manager

Objective

To practice attacking interplay starting from midfield, timing forward runs into the box with crossing and finishing.

Description

Use half a pitch and play 2 periods of 8 minutes.

Line the players up as shown in the diagram. The 3 players in the middle of the pitch play the passes as shown to finish with a shot on goal.

The same 3 players make runs into the box to try and score from a ball played in from the outside players. The first time the players try to score from 2 aerial cross from the corner of the pitch.

The next set of players use the same passing combination and try and score from a pass played in from their 2 teammates on the line. Each player should play every position.

Coaching Points

1. Encourage the players to communicate when running into the box, so they take up different positions to finish/score.

2. The cross needs to be timed well to meet the run.

Progression

Introduce defenders. The number and whether they are active or inactive should depend on the ability or age of the players.

Possession and Player Awareness Training

18 min

Created using SoccerTutor.com Tactics Manager

Objective
To improve passing, receiving, creating space and awareness.

Description
We use a 30 x 30 metre square divided into 2 areas. We change the rules around in this drill often to keep it as dynamic as possible.

The players control with one foot and pass with the other

3 teams are split between the 2 areas with a ball between the 3 in each half. We use different variations:

1. Pass the ball between themselves moving around within half the area.
2. The same using the whole area.
3. The same as the previous 2 but they pass to a different colour.
4. Possession 6 v 3 in each half.
5. Possession 12 v 6 in the whole area.

Coaching Points
1. Create space to find the right position and angle to receive the ball.
2. Improve the speed of play by limiting the players to 1 touch when possible.
3. Players need to have their heads up with full awareness of all that is around them, making sure to avoid the other teams.
4. It is very important to coach the correct body shape to be aware of other players, especially when receiving a pass.

4 v 4 + 4 Possession Game   15 min

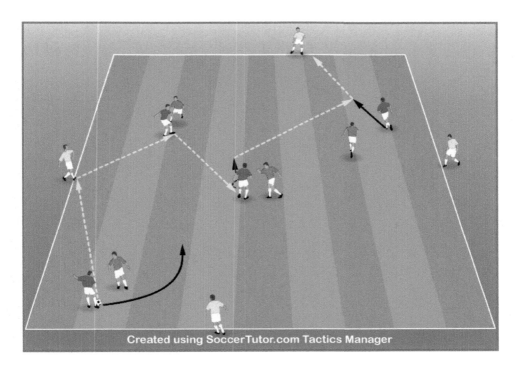

Created using SoccerTutor.com Tactics Manager

Objective
To improve possession play, passing, receiving and creating space.

Description
In a 20 x 20 metres area we play 3 periods of 5 minutes.

This possession game is 4 v 4 inside the area with the aim of keeping the ball. The 4 utility players support from the outside. Play with a maximum of 2 touches.

The outside players play with 1 touch as if they were receiving the ball with their back to goal with a marker behind.

Coaching Points
1. Play and think quickly.
2. Run into space to receive the ball and exploit the numerical advantage.
3. The defending team need to communicate to coordinate their pressing.
4. If possession is lost players need to react to the change of game situation immediately.

2 v 1 Three Zone Attacking Challenge

14 min

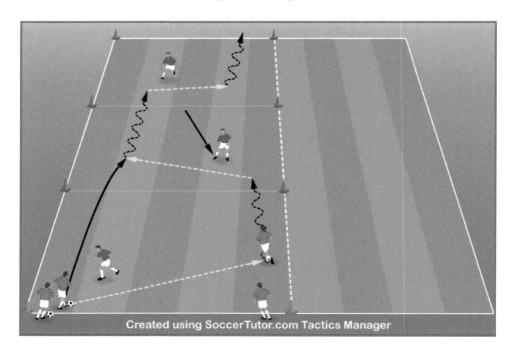

Created using SoccerTutor.com Tactics Manager

Objective
To practice playing in a 2 v 1 situation, passing and dribbling through the centre.

Description
In a 24 x 12 metre area divided into 3 parts we play 2 periods of 7 minutes

As shown in the diagram, each pair should move through each area defended by a player. The defender must wait by the line at the back of their area until the ball arrives into their zone.

Change the defenders frequently.

Coaching Points
1. Dribble the ball close to the feet so the pass can be played early.
2. Timing of the runs needs to be coordinated to the pass.
3. Encourage 1-2 combinations and make sure they are quick and sharp.

2 v 2 Dribbling Small Sided Game   12 min

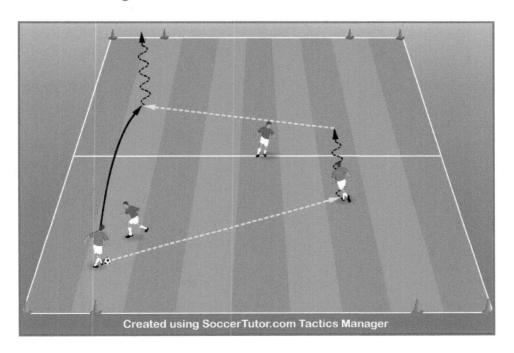

Created using SoccerTutor.com Tactics Manager

Objective

To practice dribbling, passing, receiving, pressing forward, wide play and defending.

Description

In a 20 x 12 metres area we play 4 periods of 3 minutes.

In a limited area play 2 v 2. Each team attacks and defends 2 mini goals. A goal is scored by dribbling the ball through the set of cones. To achieve this 1 of the players must have dribbled the ball across the attacking half of the pitch.

Coaching Points

1. When dribbling the players need to move the ball away from the position of the defender.
2. Players need to have explosive acceleration to beat the defender.

2 v 1/2 v 2: Attack and Defence Transition Game

16 min

Created using SoccerTutor.com Tactics Manager

Objective

To develop fast transition from attack to defence as well as dribbling and shooting.

Description

In a space double the penalty area we play 2 periods of 8 minutes.

2 teams line up as shown in the diagram. Play 2 v 1 followed by a 2 v 2 after a quick transition towards the other goal. The player defending the first action can come out when the attacking player makes contact with the ball passed by the keeper. The attacking team must play the ball backwards to their teammate on the other side.

When the first phase is over, a teammate of the defender dribbles another ball onto the field making a transition to a 2 v 2 scenario towards the other goal.

Coaching Points

1. We look for maximum speed in decision making
2. There needs to be fast transitions between attacking and defensive actions.
3. The attackers should use quick one-two combinations to get in behind the defender.
4. If there is a clear opportunity to shoot, take it quickly.

4 v 4 Fast Break Attack Game

15 min

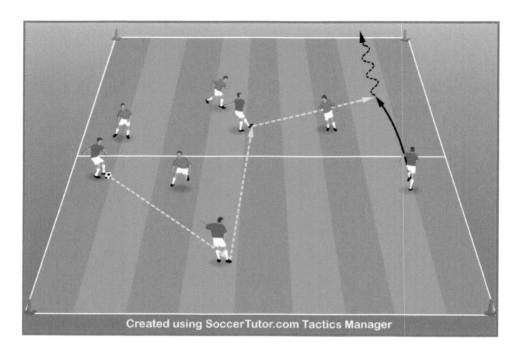

Created using SoccerTutor.com Tactics Manager

Objective
To improve dribbling, passing, receiving and fast break attacks.

Description
In a 25 x 30 metres area we play 3 periods of 5 minutes.

We play 4 v 4 in a limited area. The objective is to dribble the ball across the opposite line. To score a "goal" all of the players in the team must have touched the ball once. Play 2 touch football except when running for the line where there is no limit.

Coaching Points
1. Combinations need to be quick and sharp, utilising the space in behind.
2. Players need to create space and support the teammates.
3. When dribbling the players need to move the ball away from the position of the defender.

11 v 7 Fast Break Attacking Small Sided Game   24 min

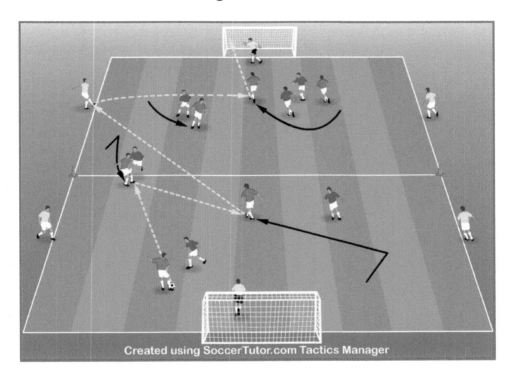

Created using SoccerTutor.com Tactics Manager

Objective
To improve quick combination play, wide play, fast break attacking and finishing.

Description
In a space double the size of the penalty area, play 3 periods of 8 minutes.

Small game with 3 teams of 6 players, with 4 utility players on the sidelines.

The attacking team must shoot on goal before they have passed the ball 4 times. If a goal comes from a pass from a utility player it scores double. Play 2 touches to encourage controlled passing.

Coaching Points
1. Players need to move into space exploiting the numerical advantage.
2. To create space to score, players need to check away from their marker.

7 v 7 Fast Wide Play Attacks and Finishing SSG

24 min

Created using SoccerTutor.com Tactics Manager

Objective

To improve attacking wide play and finishing.

Description

In a space double the size of the penalty area, we play 3 periods of 8 minutes.

Small game with 2 teams of 6 players, 4 of which are inside the playing area and 2 are outside in the attacking half. The attacking team must use 1 of the outside players before 4 passes have been made and the outside player must cross the ball.

If a goal is scored by a header from a cross from a wide utility player it is worth double.

Play with a minimum of 2 touches.

Coaching Points

1. Aim to get the ball wide as soon as possible.
2. The wide player needs to coordinate the cross to the forward runs.
3. Encourage players to move in semi-circles to get away from their marker.

3 v 3 + 3 Zonal Possession Game

15 min

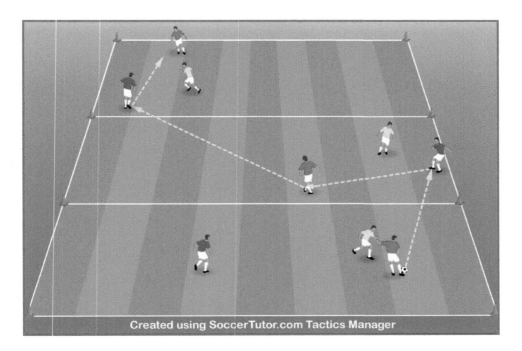

Created using SoccerTutor.com Tactics Manager

Objective
Improves control and passing, soft and hard passes with both feet, thinking before moving and execution from different areas.

Description
In a 24 x 12 metres area divided into 3 parts, we play 3 periods of 5 minutes In this possession game we have 3 teams of 3. 2 teams play against the other team. 1 player from each team is in each of the 3 zones, creating a 2 v 1 situation in each of the zones. The players may not cross into other zones trying to keep possession.

When the defending team steals the ball, they then try to keep possession while the team that lost the ball becomes the team trying to retrieve it (the defending team). Play with a maximum of 2 touches.

Coaching Points
1. Movement into space is key to exploit the numerical advantage in each zone.
2. Players should have their heads up to be aware of all passing options.
3. Speed up play by limiting the players to 1 touch.

4 v 4 + 5 Possession with 1 v 1 Break-Away Game   18 min

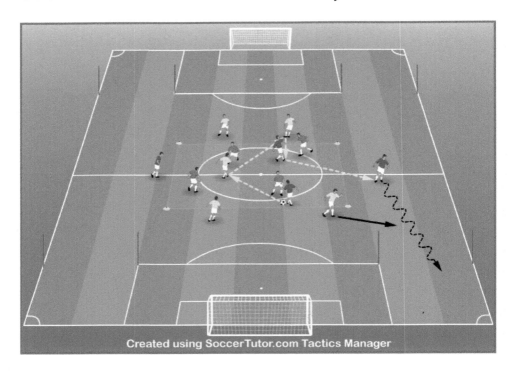

Created using SoccerTutor.com Tactics Manager

Objective
To develop passing, possession and flank play 1 v 1's.

Description
Using the area between the 2 penalty areas we play 3 periods of 6 minutes. The centre square is 30 x 25 metres.

In this 4 v 4 possession game there are also 5 utility players. 1 defending team has all 4 players inside the restricted area. The team in possession has 2 players in the restricted area with the other 2 wide outside. The team in possession also has the help of 1 utility player inside and 4 outside the zone. When they make 5 passes they play a deep pass to either of their 2 teammates giving support on the wings.

When the wide players receive the ball they dribble through the set of poles on their side of the pitch which will be defended by the opposing team's utility player producing a 1 v 1 situation. To improve the drill, the players inside the restricted area will be central midfielders, the wide players will be wingers and the 4 outside utility players are defenders.

Creating and Exploiting Space 8 v 8 Game (1)

20 min

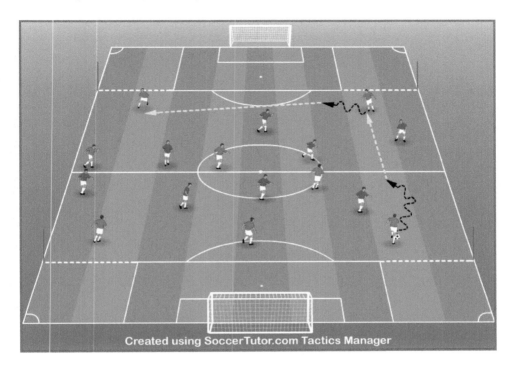

Created using SoccerTutor.com Tactics Manager

Objective
To improve players ability to create space and exploit it.

Description
Using the area between the 2 penalty areas we play 2 periods of 10 minutes.

We play possession of 8 v 8 with 2 teams. The condition is that when a player receives the ball he must touch it at least 4 times.

It is important to practice this drill in a large area to provide the space to facilitate movement and dribbling.

Coaching Points
1. Players need to dribble the ball into space.
2. Players should always be moving, creating space by losing their marker: Inside to out, outside to in, checked runs.

Creating and Exploiting Space 8 v 8 Game (2)

20 min

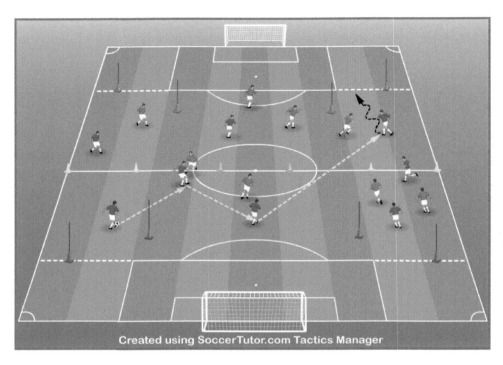

Created using SoccerTutor.com Tactics Manager

Objective
To improve players to create space and exploit it.

Description
Using the area between the 2 penalty areas we play 2 periods of 10 minutes.

8 v 8 modified game. 2 teams face each other on a pitch with 7 mini goals made from cones or coaching poles. A goal is scored by dribbling the ball through any one of these mini goals. The 3 goals in the middle of the field are neutral, so the 2 teams should focus on attacking the 2 at the other end of the pitch and defending their own 2.

Play with a maximum of 2 touches except when a player is dribbling through one of the 'goals.'

Coaching Points
1. Players should always be moving, creating space by losing their marker: Inside to out, outside to in, checked runs.
2. When dribbling to score, players should use different feints/moves to beat the defender.

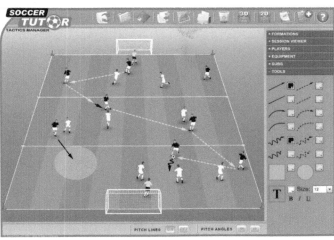

Bestselling DVDs

CPSIA information can be obtained
at www.ICGtesting.com
Printed in the USA
BVOW10s0928180517

484439BV00020B/731/P

9 780956 675262